The Anger Habit

The Anger Habit

Carl Semmelroth Ph.D.
&
Donald E. P. Smith Ph.D.

Writer's Showcase
San Jose New York Lincoln Shanghai

The Anger Habit

Writer's Showcase
an imprint of iUniverse, Inc.

For information address:
iUniverse, Inc.
5220 S. 16th St., Suite 200
Lincoln, NE 68512
www.iuniverse.com

ISBN: 0-595-14080-7

Contents

Preface

The Anger Habit has a biography as complicated as most people's lives and it would take another book to chronicle its evolution. It was born more than fifteen years ago in many conversations between the authors. Since that time it has maintained an underground life used as an unpublished version. We owe our thanks to the many people who have nourished it.

Sara Semmelroth consistently believed in the book's value and her persistent, but gentle, urging to make it more widely available was primarily responsible for its current publication. Likewise, Karolyn Smalley encouraged the book's development and eventual publication by providing enthusiastic feedback from those to whom she circulated it and her own positive and helpful suggestions.

The book has been read and reviewed by professionals from various points of view. Dale M Brethower has reviewed it as a behaviorist and Rational Emotive Therapist (RET) in all its versions. His feedback and encouragement have been invaluable. James A Bard, a RET practitioner and trainer, also gave us useful suggestions. Will Crichton lent us his extraordinary philosophical and logical skills by baring the logical bones of the theory underlying *The Anger Habit*. Hal Weidner put his English Professor's eye, as well as his lifetime study of psychological interventions at our disposal, much to the book's benefit.

One of the authors, Donald E P Smith, used an early version of the book in several graduate courses at the University of Michigan and we thank his many students for their detailed reactions. Tim Walter has also used the book with his students and his enthusiasm and advice is much appreciated.

Finally, we owe a large debt of gratitude to Louise Waller, our editor. Retired from a career of editing at several large publishing houses, she had no need to take on yet another book. Her consistently upbeat and friendly approach along with her belief in the book sustained us through many months of work, making them almost fun for the authors. Her general advice as well as her line-by-line suggestions were given in such a way as to make them consistently welcome, if not always heeded.

C.S.
August 14, 2000.

Chapter 1

The Anger Habit

As you begin reading *The Anger Habit*, stop a moment and think about your own definition of anger. The word anger, and the emotion which the word identifies, can mean a variety of things to each of us. To the authors of this book, anger is a kind of insanity in everyday life; and the hallmark of insanity is loss of self-control.

Suppose an otherwise reasonably functional man races his car around a driver who has just cut him off on the highway. Regardless of his wife and children, who are also in the car, he slams on his breaks, causing a rear-end collision with the driver of the other car. The "accident" is fatal to the man's family and himself and puts the other driver in the hospital. In the grip of anger, this man has done a crazy, destructive thing.

No other emotion plays such a disruptive role in our lives as anger. While angry, our reasoning, which is necessary for thoughtful decision-making, is impaired. While angry, we suffer a kind of insanity. Having lost the organizing power of clear perspective and reason, we are not in intelligent control of ourselves or our lives.

Anger such as this is nothing new. The written record of our civilization chronicles behaviors that are equally crazy and anger-driven. The Greek poet Homer wrote of Achilles who killed his enemy Hector and then lashed the body to his chariot and dragged it three times around the walls of the city of Troy, thus dishonoring the noble son of the king of Troy.

Anger leads to loss of control, lack of reason. No other emotion—anxiety, depression, even love—erases our control so completely.

Full-blown anger keeps us from rational direction of ourselves. As our anger increases, our intelligence decreases. But, fortunately, the reverse is also true. As our anger decreases, perspective returns, making intelligent decisions easier.

The Anger Habit is not about the control of anger. It is about the prevention of anger in our everyday lives at home, at work, at school, and at play. How we can avoid out-of-control angry behaviors by exposing our out-of-control habits is the subject of this book.

It is easy to identify an angry marriage, a friendship gone sour, a troubled parent-child relationship. When we see and hear the bickering, the lack of communication, the rudeness, the recriminations, and even the violence, we see that these relationships have been taken over by anger. If we ask the persons involved why they bicker or fight or are rude to each other, they may say something like: "She never listens to what I say. She makes me so angry!" or "He always puts me down. It makes me so mad!"

Just what exactly are we and others saying when we use explanations like these for our angry behaviors? We are saying our angry behaviors are not in our control; they are in someone else's control. And that's the way it seems to us.

The husband who beats his wife often blames her for his attacks. "She makes me do it," he'll say. Attributed blame of this kind may also be the way the victim sees the situation. A wife will blame herself for making her husband angry enough to beat her. This can be especially true with children, who are trying to figure out why they are the subjects of parental violence. What triggers this behavior on the part of a parent? What did the child do to bring on the violence?

Everyone involved in such a situation treats it as if they—not the violent person—control the violent behavior. This is especially true when the victimizer is in a rage, but it can also be true when small irritations occur.

The Anger Habit approaches angry behaviors as seeming to be out of control because they are a habit, our anger habit. **Our** habit, therefore **our** responsibility. While anger is a habit, we have little control over it. Yet we **can** change this habit of responding automatically with anger.

The book illustrates for readers how we respond with the anger habit with a number of cases of people who come to recognize their anger habit and how it affects their lives. Often they blame themselves for being angry, in a futile attempt to change their anger with more anger at themselves. These people become clients of the counselor and receive letters from the counselor that review the client's troubled behavior and the way the client deals with it. The clients are fictional composites of real clients whom the authors have worked with, and the letters illustrate typical problems brought on by the anger habit.

In these cases the reader begins to understand that the anger habit does not exist in just one narrow part of our lives. That is why the formal investigation of an individual's anger habit is often long and torturous until a liberating change can be brought about.

Parents who have damaging problems with a teenager will also have problems brought on by the anger habit elsewhere. The problems could be with a spouse or a boss when they interact with these others in an adversarial manner.

Persons who sustain the anger habit are most often also abusive to themselves. The adversarial relations with others in some parts of their lives are accompanied by an adversarial approach to themselves. And they will often respond just as badly to self-attacks as they do to attacks by others. They dig in their heels, grow stubborn even with themselves.

When we attempt to force ourselves to do the right thing through abusive self-talk—"I'm such a lousy husband. I owe it to my wife to go straight home"—we often respond as St. Paul lamented: "The good which I would I do not; but the evil which I would not, that I practice."

Changing the anger habit requires more than becoming aware of our habit of attacking. When we attempt to change this habit we are likely to start out with attacks on our own attacks. "I just called myself a lousy husband. There I go again. That's really stupid! I'm no good at this." In a complicated set of reactions, angry persons who attack themselves and are then asked to be gentle with themselves will often blame themselves for the initial attack, a no-win situation. Learning to be gentle, but persistent, with themselves is the first big obstacle that they must overcome. Much understanding and patience is needed to change the anger habit, but the rewards are enormous in the long run.

Making changes in angry interactions in one area leads to changes in other areas. Most important, the inner peace that replaces the inner turmoil of self-attack enables people to control their lives, to live with a positive sense of voluntary action.

Recognizing the anger habit in yourself and considering how to make changes can sweeten your life. Your life becomes rich with choices when you are no longer on an angry automatic pilot.

The authors hope that reading this book will help you to understand anger and enrich your choices. Freedom from habit gives freedom of choice just as does freedom from any other master. The anger habit is a particularly unpleasant and ruinous master.

The authors of *The Anger Habit* have counseled others over many years, gradually getting better at aiding others to a more satisfactory and happy life. Through the process of discovery and change, clients can let go of the anger habit. The authors have themselves changed as they worked with clients. Therefore this book is dedicated to those with whom we have worked and those whose future journeys away from the anger habit will be, it is hoped, easier and more enriching of their lives.

Chapter 2

About Anger

We are all sensitive to what life may bring us. Sam, who makes his living as a salesman, is a pro at sensing what others are preparing to do next.

Sam was in the checkout line of his local grocery when a young woman in the next line slapped her four year old. Sam had been interested by this frazzled mother and her daughter and was watching closely for several minutes because he expected the mother to end up hitting her child. He had been silently imploring the mother to "just say no!" as the child asked for candy, then reached for it, then whined, then started crying. All the while her mother said, "No." Then, "I said no!" Then, "Stop that!" And then, "You're going to get it!" As the mother's anger apparently escalated, Sam's agitation escalated. He imagined saying something to the mother, but was afraid to interfere. He felt he'd like to confront her, but thought that she didn't know much about parenting and was probably feeling miserable. Sam's anger turned to sadness.

Mary owns her own travel agency; but she, like Sam, lives her life sensing what is going on around her and within her.

Watching the same scene between mother and child from another aisle in the grocery Mary averted her eyes when the slap came. She too had seen the slap coming based on her sixty years and the experience of being a mother and grandmother. Mary's mood had changed from joyful anticipation, of shopping for her grandchildren's coming visit, to a deepening sadness, as she watched the unhappy young mother struggle with her child. Mary wanted to reach out and reassure both mother and child about the importance of love and family, and she wanted to warn them that childhood would be over all too soon. She was afraid for them, but she felt somewhat reassured when

9

she thought of people's basic resiliency and strength. In the long run the mother and her daughter would probably do fine.

Sam and Mary are both able to predict what was going to happen between the mother and her child. They can also sense where their own behaviors, thoughts, inclinations, and feelings are taking them. They both understand a great deal about anger and love and a great many aspects of their own and others' behaviors. They live among others and by themselves by sensing what is likely to happen next, as all of us do. One proof of this sense is what happens to us when we lose confidence in our ability to predict someone else's behaviors.

Suppose a person we know starts acting "crazy." We become frightened and unsure what to say or do around them. We have lost touch with our sense of what happens next, and it frightens us because we aren't sure what the result will be if we say or do the wrong thing. We don't even know what the wrong thing might be.

Sam and Mary and the young mother they were observing were all in touch, sensing what others were about to do and to some extent guiding their own behaviors accordingly. They were also guided by sensing what they tended to do. Sam felt himself wanting to confront the young mother. It was his sensing of this tendency in himself which allowed him to reconsider and take his thoughts and feelings and behavior elsewhere. He was able **not** to interfere with the mother because he was warned by sensing his anger.

It may be strange to think about your own anger as a warning signal about what you are about to do. But seeing anger in this way is a first step to preventing anger as a habit. It is our blindness to angry feelings as information that makes it so easy for us to view anger as out of our control.

Let's look at a typical example of "road rage." Henry was driving in heavy traffic when a red car cut him off.

Henry felt a sudden rush of blood to his face. "You son of a bitch. You ass hole," he yells. He slams his foot down on the gas pedal and honks his horn repeatedly. Then he pulls his car up beside the red car. Henry gives the other driver the finger. "Get the hell off the road, ass hole."

When we asked why he got so angry, Henry says that the other driver **made** him that way. His anger was expressed by honking his horn and racing to show the other driver his displeasure. Henry's wife might amend this explanation by observing that Henry gets angry all the time and has a lot of anger **in** him. "You want to watch out and not cross him," she says.

But what does it mean when we say Henry has a lot of anger in him? Why does Henry feel happy one second, then angry the next? If feelings are "in him" all the time as his wife suggests, where are they when he isn't feeling them?

Clearly when Henry is in a situation where things go in a way other than the way he wishes or expects, he assumes the task of righting the situation by attacking someone or something to make it "behave" properly. This is what his wife and friends observe in him. He responds to many situations with attacks.

"That bastard should learn to drive. Stay off the road you jerk," Henry says.

But where do Henry's feelings of anger come from and where do they go? Henry thinks his anger is a response to other people's behavior, often to his wife's behavior. He has physically attacked her during some of their arguments.

"I didn't want to hit you, but you made me so damn mad with all your nagging. You just never shut up," Henry said.

But he's not all that sure of where his anger comes from and where it goes.

"I'm so sorry. I don't know what gets into me," he apologizes.

What "got into" Henry was a sense of what he was about to do, attack his wife or someone else. Given that he is about to attack, it is perfectly normal for him to experience the anger, which goes with his preparation to attack. What isn't so normal about Henry is that he has a very bad habit of attacking people. The sense of anger is exactly that, a sense.

The point of view taken in this book is that what "is in" an angry person is the habit of attacking, not some hidden feeling lurking to break out into the open. The sense of anger is recognizing of our preparation for attack. If we habitually attack others in many different circumstances, then it follows that we will sense our preparation to attack, be angry, much of the time.

A car got in Henry's way. His immediate response was to prepare to attack the driver. His sense of anger was his awareness of this preparation.

Sam and Mary at the grocery store both saw a young mother treating her child in a way they thought was incorrect. Both their initial responses were preparing to intervene.

Sam says under his breath, "Stop that! I ought to slap **you**. What the hell do you think you're doing?"

Mary prepares to intervene in a different way. Under her breath she says, "Stop that. You're causing your own unhappiness. Please stop! Let me show you what loving can do."

Mary, Sam and Henry may all prepare to intervene when other people bother them. They have the desire to do so on occasion and the corresponding habit of intervening. But they end up responding differently.

Henry and Sam had attack responses and were made immediately aware of this by their sense of anger. Sam used his sense of anger to intervene in his own behavior.

"I'm angry. I feel like slapping that young mother. Stupid response. She just doesn't know much about parenting. Now I feel sad."

Henry also had a sense of anger, but he attributed **his** anger to the behavior of another driver. This is a mistake, which he repeats habitually. The more angry he feels, the more sure he is that someone has behaved badly. Instead of saying to himself, "I'm angry. I feel like killing that guy," Henry proceeds to "He really pisses me off. I'll teach him!"

Mary's response is to prepare to intervene, but not by attacking. Rather, her response is to prepare to give aid and corresponding to that response are caring feelings, (the sense of caring).

Neither Sam nor Mary actually ended up intervening. They both used their feelings as signals to discover what they were preparing to do and thought better of actually following through.

Henry had no such option because he viewed his sense of anger as being caused by the other driver. This gave him no alternative except to carry through with an attack or not attacking. If he did not attack it meant living with his feeling and muttering and groaning. This is what he sometimes tries to do and it makes him feel like a wimp. Quite rightly. The sense of wimpishness is the sense of being in a fight and preparing to run away. As long as Henry sees his sense of anger as caused by others rather than as a valuable signal about his own responses, he will attack others or feel like a wimp. Given the alternative of attacking or a sense of wimpishness, Henry doesn't hold back attacks very often. It is only afterward that he can sometimes see that something went wrong with his anger.

So what to do? Henry can try to "get to the bottom of my anger" by examining his past, perhaps in therapy, for the hurts which cause him to have so much anger "in him." In any case, whether he traces his anger or counters it with wimpishness, he's still stuck with a view of his own behavior which says: "Your sense of anger is caused by others and makes you do things, therefore anything or anyone who 'makes' you angry is potentially in charge of your behavior."

In an alternate view of anger—that the sense of anger tells him that he is preparing to use force—Henry is potentially in charge of his own angry behaviors and can choose alternative responses to things that bother him.

This alternative view implies that if he changes his habit of responding to others with plots and thoughts of attacking them, then his sense of anger will subside.

Two Views of Anger

Henry's View	Alternate View
Henry's wife says, "Slow down.", which **makes** him experience angry feelings, which **force** him to choose between attacking his wife and "stuffing" them and feel like a wimp.	Henry's wife says, "Slow down.", which habitually leads Henry to prepare to attack when "criticized." Henry feels these preparations as feelings of anger. They give him a chance to solve his discomfort at being criticized in some other way **before** he actually attacks.

Because we are all psychologists, we all have "theories" of anger and those theories influence our behavior. Most of us view our sense of anger as a force, which pushes against us and others resulting, if not countered, in attacks. "The devil made me do it" is often translated into "My anger is trying to make me do it."

The result of this underlying assumption, that our behavior is driven by or forced by a sense of anger, is that we act to counter or deflect that sense. Or, as the alternative, this force must be released in some way, like steam from a radiator, to keep it from destroying its container (the angry person) and damaging those near it. The resulting maneuvers—which aim at countering, deflecting, and releasing anger—themselves wreak havoc on people's lives, as we shall see in chapters still to come. The general result is a state of chronic struggle **among** people in many families and work situations and/or a state of struggle **within** people over their own behaviors and feelings.

For the authors the sense of anger is not a force, but is information. Our sense of anger is information about ourselves and the world around us. Attacks are **attempts to force** others or ourselves; the sense of anger tells us that we are preparing to force others, or ourselves, to comply with some expectation.

A major outcome of the everyday view that our sense of anger is a force is the widespread feeling that a person's behavior is involuntary. People believe that they live under conditions outside of their control and that actually doing something intentionally requires forcing themselves, kicking and screaming—or at least reluctantly—to comply with one's own intentions.

A major problem with recognizing the anger habit in ourselves is that our attacks often occur without being signaled to us with the feeling of anger. For this reason we don't see how often we respond to life's problems with attacks.

An attack is **any behavior, which has as its function an increase in discomfort of another or oneself for the purpose of control.** This description includes many behaviors as being attacks that are not usually seen in that light.

Most of us think of ourselves as attacking others only when we are victimized by their attacks, or by their selfishness or stupidity or carelessness, as when Henry felt victimized by the driver of the red car.

In fact, we spend more time attacking than we realize. We associate attacks only with temper tantrums, outbursts, or "a slow burn," and with violent and aggressive behaviors. Most of us are unaware that tears, making people feel guilty, depressive self-talk, judgmental behaviors, and name-calling can be ways in which we learn to attack others or ourselves. These are ways we increase discomfort in others or ourselves for the purpose of control. Nor do we realize that our attacks are attempts to control our own or other people's behavior by force.

The sense of anger (a signal that we are preparing an attack) is merely an indication that we are making a transition from distress to attack. Distress tells us that something isn't right, that we are in danger or that we made an incorrect prediction. It allows us to review a situation so that next time we can make a better prediction or take action to alleviate the situation. To say it another way, the feeling of distress is automatic and a necessary part of learning. But the habitual transition to attack from distress means that we characteristically attempt to reduce distress by **forcing** some change on others or ourselves.

This transition, the "anger habit," is not automatic in the sense of occurring beyond our ability to change it. The discomfort we experience when something occurs which was "not right" or "strange" or unwanted **is** automatic. But our response to this discomfort or distress does not have to be an habitual reliance on attacks so as to alleviate the "unwanted" situation.

Dealing with Distress

The Anger Habit	Choosing Behaviors
Disappointment or unwanted events cause distress, which habitually leads to attacks.	Disappointment or unwanted events lead to angry feelings, which warn us that we are preparing to attack. This warning gives us a chance to think whether we wish to carry out the attack, or consider other solutions for our problem.

Then where does the "anger habit" come from? Do we really learn angry behaviors, as the term implies? And if we do learn angry behaviors, is there anything we can do to unlearn them? Is there any way out, or are we destined to live out our days fuming and fussing, inwardly seething and outwardly scolding, gritting our teeth during the day and grinding them during the night? These are the questions we will talk about, and the answer to them is "yes."

This answer gives us cause for optimism. As children we all start with attacking behaviors. We scream and cry. We may develop and elaborate these attacks, primarily from interactive struggles with our peers, our parents, and others who try to assume control over us and over whom we seek control. We also identify with the methods of self control used by others, some of which involves the use of self-attacks. Patient, caring behaviors, can replace these behaviors.

We all employ some creative work, some play, and some uncontrolled and spontaneous interactions with others. We also do some non-interfering acceptance of our emotional lives. Even so, our tyrannical selves go on operating to some degree. Though we may not be aware of it, we go on struggling with and attacking those events—and people—that distress us, events which our expectations did not forecast. We continue to make demands on others to change the real world, to make it conform to our expected view.

But others also fight back against our attempts to control. We become extraordinarily sensitive **to** control in our struggle **for** control, as is illustrated by this interaction:

Therapist: "Joe, have you ever started to do something and had someone tell you to do it?"

Joe: "I don't know what you mean, exactly."

Therapist: "Well, suppose you spilled some coffee there on the side table, and you were just starting to reach for a tissue to wipe it up, and just then I said to you, 'There are tissues there that you can use to clean that up.'"

Joe: "Oh, yes! Now I know what you mean. I hate that! It drives me out of my tree when somebody does that! My wife does it sometimes, and it really makes me angry. Like, when I'm just starting to get up to answer the phone, she'll say, 'Dear, please get the phone.' That really ticks me off!"

Therapist: "It makes you feel like you no longer want to do what you were about to do, doesn't it?"

Joe: "It sure does. It's like she predicts what I'm about to do and then kind of takes charge of it by asking me to do it."

Therapist: "Exactly. And that makes you angry, and then you don't want to do it."

Joe: "Right!"

Therapist: "Well, Joe, you say that your main reason for coming to me is that your life seems to be made up of things you don't really want to do. You drag yourself through each day. It seems as if everything is an obligation."

Joe: "Yes, that's true. I don't even enjoy the things I should enjoy, like playing golf. What's that got to do with my wife butting in when I'm about to do something?"

Therapist: "Joe, the way you feel when you tell yourself to do things you were about to do is the same way you feel when your wife tells you to do something you were about to do. You are doing the same thing to yourself that she does to you. For example, you might notice that there are dirty dishes on the kitchen counter and say to yourself, 'I really ought to do those dishes.' Saying that to yourself may be enough to make you **not** want to do them.

"She predicts what you are about to do and turns her prediction into a demand. You predict what you are about to do, and you turn your prediction into a demand on yourself. You feel that the behavior is no longer yours in both cases. Remember, you would have willingly answered the phone if she hadn't made her prediction into a demand.

"You can live your everyday life willingly, with a sense of voluntary action, if you can stop turning so many of your observations of what there is to do into demands on yourself. In both cases the simplest things get turned into struggles. In the first case between you and your wife, and in the second case between you and yourself."

It is our observation that widespread unhappiness is produced and nourished by our attempts to reduce our distress by unthinkingly and habitually turning to attack as a solution. It is the habitual transformation of the feeling of distress into an attack or demand, which we are naming "the anger habit."

The alternatives to the automatic conversion of distress into an attack include information gathering, problem solving and learning. These alternative behaviors **free** us to be informed by and changed by the circumstances in which we find ourselves. The consequences of employing attacks inevitably trap us in struggle.

In the following chapters you will read descriptions of our attempts to help clients unlearn their anger habits. These are chronicled in the form of letters to clients summarizing their struggles to deal with their anger symptoms. The clients are not actual people, but each is a fictionalized composite representing many different actual clients seen over the past two decades. They illustrate some of the paths which can be taken in the attempt to weaken the anger habit and the resultant struggle for control, namely, how to avoid struggling for control with young children and others whose care is in our hands, and how to move away from the unhealthy, unhappy, "obligatory" living which the anger habit produces and toward the healthy, "voluntary" living to which we all aspire for a peaceful life.

Rick is the first client. He is a young man who appears to be bright, successful, on the brink of a fulfilling life. Yet he's desperately unhappy, a victim of angry habits of which he is not at all aware.

Chapter 3

Warming Up to Anger

Anger doesn't just pop up out of nowhere in an otherwise happy and peaceful life. It is practiced and incubated and kept warm by dozens of exercises performed in everyday living.

Early in the morning, Henry opened the refrigerator door and saw that he had to move the orange juice before he could get to the milk. He experienced a little distress, and thought: "Why can't she put things back where they belong? She's always doing that and I always have to pay. I'm sick of this."

Later he was getting the paper and couldn't find it near the door. He again experienced a little distress and thought: "That damn paper boy. He just throws it anywhere he pleases. Maybe I'll call up the paper and give them a piece of my mind. Maybe I'll cancel my subscription—that will fix them." He continued to think about ways to get the paperboy fired while he ate his breakfast. Later that same morning, he had an angry outburst on the highway, endangering himself and his family.

The anger habit is not just one simple habit, like always parting your hair on the left side. Like many of our habits, it is itself made up of many habits practiced in many ways in many situations.

Anyone who has tried to quit smoking knows what it's like to deal with a habit that is not just one habit. Smoking is attached to many situations and consists of all of the preparations to smoke, such as buying cigarettes and lighters and thinking about smoking. If people tried just to quit lighting up, but kept making all the preparations for smoking, they wouldn't expect much success. That is, you continue to buy cigarettes, carry them, get them out regularly, think about smoking after every meal, but just don't light up. How long would that last?

The anger habit is kept up in dozens of little ways on a daily basis. We are continually warming up to attack others by thinking critical thoughts, fantasizing about getting even, second guessing other people's behaviors, critically judging others' lives, and a host of other warm-up exercises that we practice on a daily basis. These "warm-ups" can be quite subtle, and therefore difficult to identify and change. They do not just form the fly-wheel for anger which keeps it available until it gets expressed openly in angry outbursts such as Henry's. These daily "warm-ups" affect our lives in other and in even more perverse ways.

The connection between anger and other aspects of our lives can seem distant and subtle, if we don't often actually attack others openly. When we are constantly warming up to anger, but don't often have angry outbursts, our anger is likely to be invisible to us. We are unconscious of its presence.

But the ways in which daily criticism and second-guessing manifest themselves in our lives are not hidden at all. We can become indecisive by habitually second-guessing all courses of action and our lives become dominated by a feeling of obligation. These feelings of indecisiveness and obligation in all we do are the subject of the following letter to Rick, our first composite fictional "client."

Dear Rick:

When you first came to see me, you weren't sure whether you were doing the right thing. Of course, that was one of your complaints: you never knew if you were doing the right thing. You had been going with Jill for four years, and you didn't know whether you should get married or not. You had been living in an apartment that you disliked but it was cheap, and so you didn't know if you should move. You had been working in a bank, which had nothing to do with your schooling, but you didn't know if you should quit. You were living in a small town that you thought was dull, but you didn't know if you should go to another area.

It seemed to you that the years were going by, but nothing was happening. Your life was going by, but you weren't living. You were getting older, but you didn't feel as if you were growing up. You kept asking me if you should keep coming to counseling, and, in response, I kept repeating to you what you had told me about your life. You seemed to take what I said to you—which you had told me—as a criticism of you, and that strengthened your resolve to keep coming in. Now, you had a reason. An "authority" had said you needed fixing, and so you would come and get fixed.

You then proceeded to quiz me about what was "wrong with you," what needed fixing; and I told you that you were angry and didn't know it.

You kept telling me if that is what I said, it must be true. After all, I was the expert, and if I said it, you would just have to believe it. But, of course, Rick, you didn't believe it. But then, you didn't believe much of anything. You at least had a reason for coming to counseling, and, if you were skeptical about it, it was okay because you had made me responsible, and if it didn't work out, it would be my fault.

You told me a lot of things about your background, Rick—about your insecure mother and your angry, dominating father. You told me about those scary times when you were a child, when your mother acted kind of crazy. You drew two quite different pictures of your father for me. One was of a domineering tyrant who tried to control everyone's life and who you would like to avoid as much as possible. The other view was of someone who knows everything and to whom you go with questions all the time because you respect his abilities.

I told you that I wanted you to pay attention to the way you talk to yourself because the way our parents dealt with us when we were children can be a model for how we deal with ourselves when we are adults. Whether our parents use control strategies (like making demands) or management strategies (like providing information) can serve as a pattern for the way we manage our own behavior. Your parents were into a lot of demands and threats (your father) and dire forecasts (your mother). So maybe you found it easiest and most familiar to talk to yourself by using self-attacks in the form of demands, threats, and dire forecasts.

You began to be more aware of the attacks you made on yourself to the point where you were attacking yourself for attacking yourself.

You would tell me about how, after leaving my office, you would find yourself thinking on the way home that you couldn't remember what was said, and that you're too dumb to be in counseling or that you had otherwise messed up in our sessions. Then, you would identify these thoughts you were having as self-attacks. And then, you would start telling yourself that you just had to stop attacking yourself because that was bad, and, if you really understood what I had told you and you were a good patient, you would not be attacking yourself. And, of course, Rick, these were self-attacks, too.

I reassured you that I didn't expect you to stop these attacks until you discovered more about your anger. I just wanted you to pay attention to them for now.

In our sessions you would spend a certain amount of time recounting the events of the past week. A good proportion of these events and related thoughts had to do with your job. You told me in great detail about each of your coworkers and what dull, dreary people they were. You spent at least five minutes each week on the topic of how the people of the little town where you worked were different from those living in other places. You were especially aware of their cliquishness and their mistrust of "outsiders" and their nosiness.

You were still mostly unaware of your anger at this time, and, when I pointed out to you that you were engaged in a struggle with your fellow workers and just about every customer who came into the bank where you worked, you actually almost got angry with me. You quickly saw, however, that the critical behaviors that you had been observing in yourself—of yourself—weren't just aimed at you. You were also critical of lots of other people, although it was more in the form of "mocking on them" as you put it.

The nerve that I touched which got you angry with me was a very significant one for you. When I told you that you were in a struggle with all these "ordinary" people, you heard something that you were very afraid of hearing;

*that is, that maybe you aren't aloof. Maybe you aren't "above it all." Maybe you aren't a special alien who is untouched by the people in this little town you live and work in. Maybe you are **like** them.*

From then on, you began to be very aware of the anger all around you. You began to see all the little, and not so little, attacks which people make on each other: the "kidding" about your bald spot by your fellow employees, the put-downs of customers after they leave the bank, the indignation over the "mistake" the bank allegedly made in a woman's checking account.

Then you began to be aware of the actual anger, which follows when others attack you and just before you attack them. You were helped in this by that one supervisor who you had for a short time. She was very controlling and very angry but always smiling and "very nice." She drove you to distraction by changing your schedule around, always at the last minute and for "very good" reasons. She made you squirm by giving you an endless string of advice on how to get ahead and unwanted reassurance about your failure to do so more quickly. I told you at the time that she was just what the doctor ordered, and she would be good for you. You looked at me as though I'd lost my mind. How could anybody that exasperating be good for you?

But she did us both a big favor. She helped show you your anger and its relation to control. She attacked you in very efficient and effective ways. She instinctively knew some of your most vulnerable spots. You were aloof, so she made you out to be trying to be "one of the boys." You like to know all your obligations ahead of time so that you can feel free to plan getaway time, so she kept you in suspense until the last minute about your schedule.

Your supervisor was an expert at control. She knew how to get an advantage over you and made you squirm without your being able to do anything about it. It was during this time that you began to identify your own anger. You saw that you react to anything that looks like control with some form of attack, and that this is your attempt to control others. It was with the supervisor's "help" that you got to practice a way other than counter-attacking of dealing with your own anger. We went through incident after incident of her attacks on you and your acknowledging of your anger. But, then, instead of fueling your anger by reliving your indignant reactions to her and by inventing all kinds of plans for counterattacks, we practiced diverting your attention to what could be done—to what information was needed—to problem solving rather than revenge.

*And, Rick, every time you dealt with your anger with her by saying to your-self—"I'm angry; that means I'm ready to attack to get my way," and proceeded to try to find a solution other than attacking her—you became more able to see her anger objectively, as well as your own. Now you saw her as a person who attacks others a lot in order to get her way. Despite the fact that she was out-wardly so "nice," and smiled and chatted a lot, she is an angry and attacking person. She is truly a wolf in sheep's clothing. But by now you will recognize my characterization of her as "a wolf in sheep's clothing" as **my** anger, and I can hear you laugh at that as you read it.*

We can both laugh at the way anger sneaks out of us into attacks on oth-ers, Rick, because we both know that it's just our habit of getting prepared for taking control over things and people whom we are holding responsible for what happens to us. We are warming up all the time for control, as if it is the only way to get what we want, the only way to achieve our goals. We must be in control of other people. We must be their judges and teach them a lesson when they "do wrong." If we aren't in a superior position to them by some aspect of strength or job position or legal connection, then we can, at least, set ourselves up in a morally superior position by some aspect of racial or religious or educational connection from which we can judge them. This means that when we think of them as "wolves in sheep's clothing" or "liars" or "unfair" or "jerks" or "hypocrites" or "stupid" or whatever name we call them under our breath, we are making their behavior our business. Our judgments of them are part of our preparation for trying to take charge of others by attacking them.

Rick, controlling others by attacking them is a heavy-duty job. It requires a lot of preparation. It's like getting ready for a prizefight; it requires a lot of training and a lot of warm-ups and practice. Doing exercises and roadwork and stretches don't look much like fighting. But they are activities the fighter does to get ready for a fight. Judgments and aloofness and self-talk consisting of criticisms don't look much like control of others either. But they are part of how we warm up to anger.

Then, Rick, I asked you to go a step further with me. This step was to realize that you do not need your self-importance any longer. Self-importance is something very different from self-esteem or specialness. Your specialness is not something you need to protect or foster and certainly not something you need to get rid of. That "thing" which you have been protecting by your aloofness and your preparation for counterattacks on whoever attacks you is merely your self-importance. Self-importance, Rick, is just the opposite of specialness.

Self-importance makes you vulnerable to anyone who comes along. You are vulnerable because your self-importance consists of the view of you that you want others to have. It is the face you wear reflecting the person you would like to be, a person who is entitled to control others.

Rick, up to now we have focused on your response to others' attempts to control you, and your attempts to control them. We have driven a wedge between your anger response and your attacks on others. We have taken a habit, the anger habit, and changed it. When you become upset now, you don't automatically attack. As a consequence your anger gets a chance to drift away without the reinforcement of your attacks, which have usually followed it.

Then, we looked at your preparation for attacks on others. Self-importance, Rick, is a preparation for control of others. Self-importance is the armor, which someone must have if he or she is going to attack others without their being able to retaliate. It is the symbol of office, which seems to entitle a person to control others. It is the king's crown, the jurist's black robe, the physician's white coat, and the teenager's sports car.

In the children's story of the emperor who wore no clothes, it was self-importance that supposedly clothed him. What the emperor wore was important because his regal appearance was a part of what lent him authority as a lawmaker for others. Without his clothes, he was without the power he needed to control his subjects. Without your self-importance, you are lacking the authority to judge and condemn others for violating your expectations—which you treat as "proclamations."

And just as the emperor (without his imperial robes) was powerless and vulnerable to humiliation by a child who merely observed that he wore no clothes, so you are vulnerable to humiliation by anyone who comes along and utters the most ordinary observation such as, "You have a bald spot," or "I can see that you want to get ahead in the bank, so you should go to this special course on real estate. " You were vulnerable to these remarks because they punctured the aloof front you present to others, the face, which implies that you are in control of the world.

Rick, it is a common belief that people put up fronts for others in order to protect themselves in some way. And that's the way it seems because, when our "fronts" are breached or even punctured a little, we experience discomfort. Now that you recognize your anger better, Rick, you will be able to see that these fronts are built and maintained as a means for attacking, controlling, and dominating others. Yes, we need the front for protection. But we need protection only to prepare for control of others.

Stockades were built by settlers to protect them from hostile natives. But they needed protection only because they wanted to take land and wealth from those people. They needed the stockades in order to control the area around them. The earlier traders didn't need stockades and forts because they traded value for value. They did not see themselves as entitled to what they wanted by self-important proclamation. And that is our model for dealing with others without our "fronts." If we can deal with others around us as a trader, giving value for value, then we do not need our self-importance.

It is only when we want something from others that we feel we cannot earn that we need our self-importance. I said before that a sense of specialness, of self-esteem, is the opposite of self-importance. And now you can see why this is. A sense of specialness comes with our perception of our own value. A sense of our value is what allows us to interact with others as a trader. It is the necessary condition for a productive business, a productive *profession, and a productive worker. It is also the condition for a productive relationship. It fosters intimacy with others who are different from us.*

Self-importance does just the opposite. It produces exploitative relationships. The doctor or the banker who decorates his waiting room with mahogany feels justified in charging exorbitant fees, not because of his specialness but because of his membership in a special group. The man who proclaims undying love to his lover and asks, in exchange, her eternal fidelity is about to exploit her. He is unsure of his own worth and tries to exact a promise in order to bind her to him with a vow of fidelity. The doctor or the banker is proclaiming a worth they do not feel. The lover is proclaiming knowledge of the future that he, in fact, cannot have. He is trying to exchange what he does not have for a value he does not feel he can earn, his lover's devotion.

Rick, up to now in therapy you have been tracking down your anger in order to identify it when it occurs, and not to feed it by attacking others or yourself. You are doing this nicely. You are able to say, "I'm angry," and let it go at that. Now I'm asking you to notice the nature of the attacks on you that make you angry. In order to do this I want you to ask yourself whenever you feel anger, "What do I want that I feel I can't earn?"

When a customer at the bank treats you curtly and asks to see someone with some authority, you will become angry. Ask yourself then, "What do I want from this customer?" I think you will find that what you want is for that person to treat you as though he valued you, to show you deference. And then ask, "Do I need this customer to value me just because I'm here, representing the bank, or can I earn my own way?" I know you will find, Rick, that you can earn your own way in life without having to have every stray person with whom you come into contact treat you as a valuable person just because you are you.

Rick's early years, as is true of many of us, were a training ground for habits which restricted his choices of behavior in later life. Counseling was a process of developing choices in his life to replace automatic responses driven by these early habits. Rick's parents used demands, threats, and dire forecasts to try to keep him under their control. He used cries for help and demonstrations of confusion to control them and "sucker" them into being responsible for whatever happened to him, especially when that something was bad. An alternative strategy would have been to provide him with information and to allow him to make more of his own decisions, right or wrong. As an adult, when Rick was upset, he tried to bring himself under control by using demands, threats, and dire forecasts. He was sometimes able to direct his anger at others when they did something that clearly meant that they were not looking out for *his* interests. For example, his landlord raised his rent from $500 per month to $600. Rick was shocked and scared and angry.

Rick's Response Choices

Rick's Response

"Sonofabitch! Money grabbing landlords! What can I do? I'll tell him it isn't fair. I've been a good tenant, and he can't do this to me! But he'll say he's just following orders. And then he might get pissed and give me rotten service. Then, what can I do? I'll tell him to stick it, give notice and find a cheaper place. But what if I can't find one? Then I'll be out on the street. I'd better just shut up and pay. But I can't afford it! That's my bosses' fault. I'll tell the boss he has to give me a raise. But he might decide he's paying me too much

Alternative Response

"That makes me angry!...OK, what can I do? I could talk with the super, see what he has for $500."

The super tells him that there's nothing else available, and part of the increase is to hire a night security guard.

"What else can I do? I can pay the rent and start looking for a cheaper place. Or I could offer to work one night a week as a guard for $100 a month. What else can I do? I can talk with my boss about my future prospects at the bank and maybe find out when a raise is due. Or I could already and fire me.

"What's the matter with you, Rick? You just let people push you around, take advantage of you. Be a man! Face up to those suckers! Quit your job and let 'em find out what they're missing!"

He takes out the trash and manages to miss the dumpster. Most of the trash falls on the ground.

talk with Jill about sharing an apartment."

He talks with his boss and finds out that they're planning to open a branch in two months. They've been considering him for either head cashier at the branch or a transfer with a raise in pay. He talks with Jill about looking for a larger place that they can share.

As Rick began to recognize his anger and to name it, he increased the likelihood that his next behavior will be reasoned rather than habitual. As he became more skillful at recognizing anger, he also began to recognize his "anger habit" and its use in his struggle to control others. For example, his response to the following situation was easily seen by him to have an alternative which was much more satisfying to him. Recognizing alternatives to the habit of responding with demands is a big step toward reducing the strength of the anger habit.

Therapist: "What did your supervisor say when you asked for the extra hour on lunch break?"

Rick: "She said, No! (Dumb idiot!) Said, if the Motor Vehicle Bureau is closed on Saturday, I should pay by mail. She doesn't understand it's a bum rap and I need to make 'em see that."

Therapist: "What went through your head when she said 'No'?"

Rick's Response Choices

Rick's Old Response	Alternative Response
"I had a vision of throwing her through the window. I was afraid it'd kill her. It felt terrible. Christ, Rick, you're acting crazy! Get a grip on yourself, screwball! This idiot is killing me and I can't fight back. What kind of man are you? Take charge! Get control of yourself. Get on top of this situation! Ah-h-h." (A feeling of depression follows.)	"I was really mad! She makes me so damn mad! She's trying to control me. "Oh, and I'm whipping myself into a frenzy in order to control her! "Okay. So what's the problem? "I want to tell those people that the meter was broken. I tried to pay the meter and it wouldn't work. "But that means taking a business day off. So, I should go ahead and pay my three bucks. I'll write a note and explain it. "Then the ball's in their court."

Rick's unhappiness with his life was traced to his chronic anger, of which he was unaware. His inability to accept or value his co-workers stemmed from his habitually critical view of other people. His chronic anger, just below awareness, made him sensitive to the flaws in others, which he then used to account for his unhappiness in his work. His supervisor was an expert at subtle bullying (attacking him where he was most vulnerable), and so she could control and dominate him. His lack of awareness of the reason for his own aloofness made it possible for his boss to attack him while he remained blind to her abuse, even as he was suffering from it. Since he was unaware of his anger, he was unaware that she was attacking him, and was unable to devise a rational way to escape the bullying.

Again, as Rick became aware of his own angry responses, *as* angry attacks that perpetually went nowhere, he became freer to devise creative and constructive alternative solutions to his everyday problems. Instead of being paralyzed by the distresses at work and at home, he was able to act in ways that actually solved problems.

As problem solving began to replace his anger habit, Rick benefited from the changes he made in his behaviors at home and at work. The sense he had of nothing happening in his life and the low level depression he had experienced for years began to lift.

On one occasion Rick reported that a new teller had been hired, an eighteen-year-old girl who had just graduated from high school. The head teller had taken Rick aside and said, "Rick, I want you to train Rena. She's the old man's niece, so treat her with kid gloves. You cash in and out as usual, but put in as much time with her as you need to keep her out of trouble."

Rick's Response Choices

Rick's Old Response

"What the hell do I do now? They expect me to do my own job and hers! And if she messes up, I'm the one who gets the blame.

"Why are they doing this to me? A-h, they're setting me up, expecting me to mess up so they can fire me, replace me with this kid. But I'm the best teller they've got!

"Gee, these people must be

Alternative Response

"I feel angry, really imposed on! Well let's see. What do I do? Wow, this is scary. I've never trained anyone before. But then, who else could they ask? I'm the logical person, the best teller they've got. They showed good judgment.

"Now let's see. First, I'll make a list of the standard procedures. Then I'll do the calculators and stupid. They refuse to believe that I know more about this operation than they do. If they respected me, they wouldn't do this to me. And look what they give me, a piece of fluff, still wet behind the ears.

"She looks like she doesn't have a brain in her head. Well, let's see if she can count to ten."

After two weeks Rick reported that Rena had been assigned to another teller. He predicted that she'd be "fired within a month."

computers as we come to them. But that will slow down service and customers might complain.

"Okay. I'd better work out some simulations first. We won't take customers until the third day.... Hey, why didn't they train me this way?"

The head teller commented that Rena must be very bright to have learned so fast. Rick agreed. He decided it would be good for everybody to have them be proud of his trainee. He saved his simulation exercises to use in a training program he might construct in his spare time and present to the head teller.

The case of Rick will continue in Chapter Eleven. There, his case will demonstrate the liberating effects of freedom from the anger habit. As he makes his way out of the web of his own anger he begins to experience his actions differently, an experience the authors call "voluntary living."

Chapter 4

A Tool of Anger

Now meet Leslie, the mother of teenage Sally. Leslie is feeling miserable. She thinks her misery is caused by her teenager's behavior, that's the way it feels to her. Leslie's struggle with Sally over her daughter's behavior is accompanied by anger, tears, and guilt, and dominates Leslie's life. She is miserable, she thinks, because she is unable to control Sally and that makes Sally in control of her misery.

But Leslie will find out that, contrary to what she has been led to believe; her misery is under her own control. In fact, without knowing it, her misery has become her major tool for attempting to control her daughter.

Dear Leslie:

You've told me how frustrated you are with your daughter, Sally, how you lose your temper, how you would just as soon she would find somewhere else to live, how you slap her when she mouths back, and all the rest. Your physician sent you to see me because of your continual and severe stomach and intestinal problems, which the doctor thinks might be due to stress. I don't know if that is true or not. We won't know that until you are able to live your life differently so that you are less unhappy. In the meantime, your physician may find something she can treat which might be contributing to your stomach problems. Or it may be some combination of both.

*In any case I'm going to help you get started ridding yourself of stress. In order to do that, I'm going to ask you to do something that will sound very simple, but will be very hard to carry through. I'm going to ask you to start dealing with your anger and frustration with your daughter as **your** problem, and to see your daughter's behavior as a separate problem.*

In order to separate your anger problem from Sally's behavior problem, I want you to do two things: First, when you are angry with her because of her behavior, I want you to say aloud, "I'm angry." And, second, I want you to wait to decide what to do about Sally's bad behavior until your anger has subsided.

I will teach you what to do about Sally's bad behavior and help with your parenting later, but right now I want you first to acknowledge to yourself when you are angry, and second not make parenting decisions while you are angry.

What you are doing is this: You are trying to control your daughter's behavior with your emotions; that is, with your distress and your anger. I'm using words like "control" and talking to you about your anger in a way that you might find offensive. But I'm not accusing you of anything. I'm describing to you something that all of us do and that leads us to undesirable results when we do it.

The reason we all try to control someone else with our emotions at times is because we were all two years old at one time. There isn't any adult alive, including you and me, who wasn't two years old; and so we all have available to us the behaviors we used back then. So I'm not accusing you. I'm simply describing to you a natural set of events which occur and which you can do something about. There isn't anything you do that isn't natural; and it will help you to change your behavior if you join me in viewing it as natural instead of willful and bad.

Now, back to when we were small children. When we are born, and until we learn to use abstract language, we communicate with our parents and others by using signals. When we are disturbed by pain or other discomforts, we signal this discomfort by demonstrations, which make our parents uncomfortable. We scream and cry. No baby is born with chimes that pleasantly signal feeding or changing is required. No, the baby's "signal" is an aversive, noxious sound that others find difficult to ignore. Parents respond to our signal because it makes them uncomfortable when we are uncomfortable. But notice, the baby appears to be miserable when sending these signals. A crying baby or a two-year-old having a temper tantrum are not poster children for a happy life.

*Don't think that our parents just respond in order to feel comfortable. If this were all there was to it, all babies would have a short life. Our parents view **us*** as being uncomfortable, and it is **our** discomfort that they view as causing **their** discomfort. In the same way, when parents view us as happy, they feel good and they credit their happiness to our happiness. This is a very important point, which we will come back to many times in different contexts. It is what we may call the "objectification of emotions" and it is the basis of how we value people and objects.

This process of feeling emotion outside ourselves is what is called "empathy" when we are talking about other people. But it is a broader phenomenon than that. We do the same thing with art objects, music, and thousands of objects and events in our lives. This is the process by which we perceive value and beauty in our world, instead of just pleasure and pain in ourselves. When viewing a painting we credit our good feelings to the painting itself, to **its** beauty. We use awareness of our emotional responses first as a bridge to the emotional lives of other people and second as a measure of the value and beauty of objects.

But, for now, let's get back to the way we controlled our parents with displays of misery before we learned abstract language. As we got older and learned language and, therefore, began to be able to conceptualize what was going on between us and our parents, we thought our emotions (our expressions of discomfort) make other people do things, at least some of the time. And we found that we also responded to our parents' anger or emotional demonstrations. This in turn led us to "see" that other's "needs" (emotions) could make us do things, at least some of the time.

Often we were shown that the response of others to us, or our response to others, depended on the intensity of the demonstration of distress. Crying harder or screaming more or getting angrier (which are all the same thing) resulted in a response from others when milder measures had failed. It began to look to us as if the more we demonstrated that we wanted something, the more likely we were to get it. "Wanting" literally means to demonstrate our distress over not having something.

Through this process we begin to believe that we, and others, have a will, which moves other people. Then they in turn can move us with their will. In *the case of conflict between our "will" and our parents' "wills," who wins comes down to who is stronger "willed." This in turn comes down to who is going to threaten more, cry more, and be more distressed for the longer time.*

Fortunately, abstract language continued to develop and bore fruit for us way beyond these initial conceptualizations of willful interaction with others. You learned to solve problems in a thousand ways beyond just "putting your 'will' against" the world by having some version of a temper tantrum. You learned to abstract your world so that you could problem solve by thinking and by saying, "What if this were different; then I wouldn't have this problem." In short, you learned to use information to solve problems rather than to use temper tantrums and "will power."

All of us have a legacy of this early learning and we tend to revert to our emotional demonstrations in certain situations. This is the case when we inter-act with others in parent-child-like situations. Any situation that seems to include dominant-submissive roles may be viewed as a parent-child interac-tion. Teacher-student, employer-employee, customer-store employee are only a few examples. The situations in which people tend to "regress" to emotionally based interactions are in schools, at work, in marriage (when viewed as a dom-inant-submissive relationship), and, of course, when we rear our own children.

Leslie, it is not an accident that the two areas of your life where you have experienced extreme stress are with your work after a new boss was hired and started making changes without consulting you, and with your daughter. In both of these areas you regressed to a mode of interaction based on your will against theirs, which comes down to your misery against theirs. In both areas you viewed any problem between you and them as having one of two out-comes: Either you would win and would be in control and happy; or they would win and leave you defeated and miserable, sick, helpless, and without hope. These two situations produce in you a two-year-old view of yourself, a view that assumes you are either a lovable person whose misery matters to adults and they therefore comply with your wishes; or you are an unloved, neglected person who is powerless because your misery doesn't matter to either your daughter or your boss.

Leslie, notice how your arguments with your daughter progress. She does something like come home late. You declare how worried and frantic you are. She declares you make her miserable. You tell her how terrible your life is being made by her. And on and on. You both go into a contest. Who is the most miserable? And the winner is the biggest victim of the other's behavior.

Now, back to what we are going to do about this. We are not going to tell you—"Leslie, grow up and behave like an adult." I'm not saying that to you and I don't want you to say that to yourself when you get angry with your daughter. That is just a way of getting angry with yourself and attacking yourself with the two-year-old method.

*All I want you to try to do for now is to acknowledge that you are angry when you **are** angry, and not to try to do anything about your daughter's behavior **while** you are angry. By learning to do this, you will gradually unlearn the habit of jumping into the contest of "who is the most miserable?" every time Sally does something which upsets you.*

It will be helpful for you to monitor your thoughts about Sally even when you aren't with her. Try to recognize that the scary thoughts you have about what she's doing and how she's going to end up in life are leading you into the misery you are apt to proclaim to her when you see her. We will be talking about more effective ways of influencing Sally's behavior later. But in order to influence her behavior effectively, your interventions cannot be done angrily or out of your unhappiness. The one best thing you can do for your daughter is to stop yourself from being miserable. You have told me that you don't remember your own parents as being very happy while you were growing up. You always felt as if they were putting their unhappiness on you. Now you can break that cycle. You can learn to let go of the misery you use to feed your attacks on your own daughter.

Look at this scenario. Sally is late! It is almost one o'clock in the morning and she promised she'd be home by midnight! Leslie is on her fourth cup of coffee, and her hand is trembling, a combination of nerves and caffeine. "Is that a police car? (She has a vision of a car crash with Sally being lifted out, blood gushing.) No, it's an ambulance. (She has another vision of the hospital emergency entrance, a gurney being pushed down a hall carrying Sally's broken body!) What can I do? I shouldn't have let her go to that party! I'll bet they're drinking and doing drugs. (She has a vision of Sally reeling down a hallway to a bedroom, where some boy mauls her.)"

The front door opens and closes quietly.

Sally comes in and says "Oh, Mom! You're still up?"

Leslie's Response Choices

The I'm Miserable Response

Leslie: "Don't 'Oh, Mom' me, young lady. Where have you been? Sneaking in here at all hours of the night! No wonder I don't trust you."

Sally: "You always think the worst. You have an evil mind."

Leslie: "Almost two hours late and I'm sitting here, worried to death, about to call the police and the hospitals. What do you mean staying out half the night, at your age? You've been drinking, haven't you?

"Come here! Let me smell your breath. And carousing around with those high school jocks! Well? What do you have to say for yourself?"

Alternative Response

Leslie thought "Thank God she's safe!"

Leslie: "You're forty-seven minutes late."

Sally: "Oh, I know. Anne's father insisted on driving all of us home. And I was the last one to get dropped off. I didn't think it would take over an hour."

Sally: "Smell all you want.
Why don't you call the police.
I'm such a criminal."
Leslie: "Well, you're
grounded for a month! How do
you like that? Now, get to bed
before I thrash you!"

Leslie started trying to recognize her anger in a systematic way and was able to see her life in a less miserable light. She began to see that her misery was a handmaiden to her control struggle with her daughter. Leslie had assumed that being unhappy was **her job as a parent** when her daughter misbehaved.

The cultivation of misery, usually in the form of viewing ourselves as victims, is a necessary part of the well-honed anger habit. Anger does produce misery in family relationships. But family members cultivate their own feelings of misery so they can use them to attack and counter others' attacks. Misery is a tool of their anger.

Managers and workers can cultivate unhappiness in work places. If managers and/or workers attack each other habitually, they will cultivate their posture of being a victim and use misery in chronic preparation for attacking one another. In the workplace misery is easily cultivated by managers who believe their jobs are to be unhappy with workers' miscues, just as Leslie thought it was her job as a parent to be unhappy with her daughter's unacceptable behaviors.

Leslie was also involved in a struggle with her manager at work and was miserable there as well. She and her boss were in a contest over which one was made more miserable by the other.

It is imperative for Leslie to recognize her anger before she is able to give up fanning her attacks on Sally with her own unhappiness. Emotionality must not automatically lead Leslie to prepare to attack Sally if Leslie is going to be able to respond more constructively to her daughter.

Crucial to this process is that Leslie understand the role her unhappiness plays in her attempts to control her daughter. **Leslie tries to use her unhappiness to punish Sally and so control her.** Leslie stocks up on her misery so she can control both her daughter and her manager at work. Leslie sometimes succeeds in stockpiling misery and when Sally sees her mother is unhappy, Sally expects to be attacked for doing something wrong. Expectancy (prediction) of pain or other forms of dissatisfaction **cause** dissatisfaction, usually in the form of dread or fear. When Leslie becomes unhappy, her daughter experiences dread or fear.

This is why displaying misery and unhappiness is a tool that can be used to control the behavior of others. Others recognize our displays for what they are, our preparation to attack them. This works because it results in discomfort in those our displays target caused by their anticipation of discomfort. This in turn leads to their attempts to alleviate that discomfort. It is those attempts of others to alleviate their distress (stemming from our signs of anger) that we then see as "under our control." This is because the dread or fear which other people feel and attempt to escape by placating us, results from **our** angry feelings and/or behaviors or other displays. The link between our anger and other's dread is the causal connection between our feelings and displays of anger on the one hand and the behaviors of others on the other hand. **It is the source of our sense of willful control over others.**

If Sally always submitted to her mother's unhappiness with her, as some children do, she would likely grow up like Rick in the previous chapter. She would live her life wondering whom to please next, with unrecognized anger, and with the sense that her actions and decisions don't really belong to her.

We would all like others whom we love to respond caringly to our unhappiness. Leslie is no exception. She would like Sally to care about her and love her. What she cannot have is control over Sally's caring and still feel that it is given lovingly. As long as she continues to **use** her unhappiness to control her daughter, Sally will most often recognize it for what it is, an attempt to control her. And Sally doesn't often submit to her mother's displays. Instead, Sally is apt to respond with an even greater display of distress than her mother's. So we have two people attempting to trump each other with the degree of their unhappiness.

On occasion Leslie or Sally become really creative, or "lucky," and each sometimes "wins" a round. They succeed in winning the battle of "Who's the one with the most emotional hurt?" A "win" occurs when one of them is successful in being upset enough or hurt enough to make the other one surrender.

Conquest by Misery

A "Win" for Leslie

Leslie: "Sally! How many times have I told you? Clean up that filthy room of yours!"

Sally: "You're always nagging me about my room. Judy was over here the other day and she said she really felt sorry for me having to put up with you."

Leslie: "I'm so sorry for you having to put up with me. Maybe you won't have to much longer." Leslie turns away sadly.

Sally: "Mom? What's the matter?"

Leslie: "Oh. Nothing. I found a lump in my breast the other

A "Win" for Sally

Sally: "Mom, will you run me over to school? I'm late for cheerleading."

Leslie: "Sorry. I'm late for an appointment. If you'd be more responsible you wouldn't make me late all the time. I worry that you'll never be able to keep a job."

Sally: "But Mom, I just have to be there on time." Sally starts crying.

Leslie: "Sally? What's the matter?"

Sally: "Oh. Nothing. I feel so bad. All the other girls have rich day. It's probably nothing. But I guess I ought to call the doctor for an appointment."

Sally: "Oh Mom. I didn't know. I'm so sorry."

Later, Sally starts cleaning up her room, feeling scared and tearful.

parents. I don't feel like they accept me. I couldn't stand it if Ms. Holly made an example out of me for being late."

Leslie takes her to practice and feels awful all evening.

By learning to recognize her anger and how she cultivates her own misery as a weapon, Leslie is on her way to unlearning her anger habit. Her first comment to giving up her immediate angry response to Sally is: "You mean I'm just supposed to let her get away with that?" The words "let her" raise the question of who is in control of Sally's behavior. When she thought about this, Leslie began to see that, really, Sally is in control of her behavior. And, further, that's the way it ought to be. After all, Leslie wants her daughter to be responsible and do the right things because Sally sees they are the right things. Leslie doesn't want her daughter to "behave" just because her mother will feel bad if she finds out about Sally's misbehavior.

So how can Leslie parent? How can she influence her daughter without trying to wrestle with her over control? Could she control her daughter using some other method? The answer to this question is the subject of our next chapter.

Chapter 5

Struggling for Control

The attempt to control the behavior of others by using distress not only stimulates distress in the targeted person but it also makes for distress in the controlling person. This involves increasing misery in both oneself and those we seek to control.

What about other forms of control such as calm, cool threats? Would they be less distressing to Leslie? Here Leslie and her daughter, Sally, help us to see what control is all about. What do we need to do to control someone else? Is it really what we want?

Dear Leslie:

You are beginning to acknowledge your anger, and so are beginning to separate the problem of being angry from problems you have with your daughter's behavior. Part of the difficulty in making this separation is the fact that you know no other way of approaching Sally's behavior problems than to attempt to control her. In order to help you further in separating your anger from Sally's bad behavior, I will teach you another approach to your daughter's troubles besides your attempt to control her by showing unhappiness with her.

First, let's look at your interaction with Sally the way it now occurs. Take the incident that you were upset about last week. She brought home a report card with two F's and three D's. This was after she had assured you for the last several weeks that she was doing better in biology—for which she received one of the F's—and that she was doing fine in all her other classes. You became angry and told her, among other things, that she was good for nothing, a liar, was going to be a welfare bum, and that she was probably going to get pregnant and drop out of school. Sally got angry and upset and then cried and told you that that you never believe her, so why tell you the truth? You don't trust her to be "good," so why shouldn't she screw around? She has messed around with boys, so what? You slapped her and screamed that you wish she'd find a friend to live with, and that you wish you had never been a mother.

Now, Leslie, I've stressed to you that we are going to look at your behavior as natural and without moralizing by either of us. Interactions like this one with your daughter are natural. They occur for very good reasons. We will not change them by calling them bad and trying to make you feel bad about them. You already feel bad, anyway. So don't attack yourself about what happened and you will see, after a while, that you can trust me not to attack you about it. It is my job to convince you that the way to change these interactions, if you want to change them, is to understand them. Just wanting to change isn't enough.

Let's look at what happened and try to understand the interaction. It will help us to see why this kind of interaction takes place if we look at it as you have said it always is. You have said that you and Sally have always had a battle of wills. Since she was two years old, it has been your will against hers. What does it mean to battle another person's will? Leslie, you have always been aware that you want Sally to "mind you." Now I'm asking you to think through with me what this means.

You want Sally to do what you want her to do. It would be even nicer if she would want to do what you want her to do, even if she doesn't want to do it. Sounds kind of funny doesn't it? But it really does capture what you would like, even though it's a contradiction to say she should want to do something even if she doesn't want to do it.

What you want can be stated another way. You want to control what Sally does whether she likes it or not. So it makes sense that if what you want is to control Sally, probably many of your interactions with Sally represent your attempts to control her. We will look at what happened between you last week as if taking control is what you were doing.

Now, it looked to you as if you just had an outburst, then lost your cool and reached your wit's end. But, as I said before, we are going to look at it as a natural occurrence, as something that is inevitable, given the way you viewed it at the time. That doesn't mean that these interactions must continue to happen. That's why we must understand them; so they are no longer inevitable.

What does it mean to control someone? It means more than our being a cause of their behavior. If you drive your car over the speed limit, you may cause the police to give you a ticket, but you wouldn't say you controlled the officer's behavior. If you fix a good meal Sally may enjoy it, but you wouldn't be in control of her enjoyment. We interact with dozens of people every day, which is to say, we do things that cause them to behave in certain ways, and they do things that affect our behavior. We influence each other. But we don't control others and they don't control us. So, again, what does it mean to control?

To control someone means that we cause someone to do something, which we want them to do whether they want to or not. They have no way to counter our attempt to make them do as we wish. They must do as we want or suffer bad consequences that they will not be willing to accept. "Your money or your life" is that kind of choice.

*Now, there are basically two ways to cause someone to decide to do something or to decide to stop doing something. We can give them some information about how doing something (or not doing it) will be pleasant for them. This is called **prediction of reinforcement**. Or we can give them some information about how doing something (or not doing it) will be hurtful and/or injurious to them. This is called **prediction of punishment**. Notice that both of these ways of causing others' behavior to change voluntarily are really ways of giving them information.*

If we tell someone, "Your house is on fire," we are causing his or her behavior to change. They immediately take appropriate action. But we aren't controlling their behavior.

If we tell someone that he can get a bargain on a CD player through a mail order catalogue, then we are affecting his behavior. He may go and look at the price, but his behavior isn't under our control.

But what if we tell someone that if she doesn't give us $10,000 we will set her house on fire? Then that person's subsequent behavior may or may not be controlled by us, depending on what recourse she has. If she is able to get the *police to stop us, or is able to restrain us in some way, then we do not control her. Notice that we still influence the person's behavior. By calling the police she struck back at us, and this retaliation was due to our threat against her.*

So you see, Leslie, controlling others' behavior isn't the same thing as influencing it. Both influence and control involve giving others information which has an effect on their behavior. But control means that not only does the behavior change but the person has no way of forestalling the (bad) consequences, which our information predicted, other than to do as we demand. The person must be powerless to change our behavior by attacking us.

Leslie, we are now in a position to see what it really means to describe your interactions with Sally as a "battle of wills." You and Sally have always battled for control of each other's behavior. "To control" means that one must be in a position to attack without effective interference. This implies that for you to control Sally you must be able to tell her (give her information) that she will be hurt or injured; and she must not be in a position to stop you from inflicting hurt by attacking you or by otherwise escaping your attack. The same is true for her in reverse. She must be able to hurt you to stop your attacks (influence your behavior) and also be invulnerable to your attempts to stop her counterattacks on you (and so control you).

When two people are attempting to control each other, they are always doing two things. One is attacking or threatening to attack the other; the second is trying to make oneself invulnerable to counterattack.

What happened in your blowup last week?

First, you saw Sally's grades and attacked her by forecasting that she would become a bum.

Second, she got angry and told you that you are untrusting and a bad mother.

Third, you slapped her and said she made you wish you weren't a mother.

In this incident both of you were trying to control the other by attack and by establishing invulnerability. You and Sally both attacked by name-calling. She attempted to establish her invulnerability by disowning you as a parent, which also functioned as an attack on you. You attempted to establish your invulnerability by slapping Sally, which communicated that because you are bigger, you can hurt her and she has to take it. You also tried to establish your invulnerability by "disowning her," which says, "You can't accuse me of being a bad parent because you're not my child."

*Leslie, you can begin to see now why I insist that your interactions with Sally are natural. You have always been led to believe that, as a parent, you need to control your child. Most people say that. Other parents (yours, for example), teachers, some psychologists say it. In some cities parents are even held legally responsible for their children's misbehavior. You must be in charge of your child's behavior. So you have been trying to establish control. In doing so you have been doing all the right things and doing them quite naturally. If you are going to control Sally, you do have to promise her hurtful consequences and put her in a position where she cannot avoid them. This means you must attack her in ways that do not allow her to defend herself, which means she cannot attack you. When she succeeds in counterattacking, as she did here, you worry about losing control. **As long as you view control over Sally as your goal, these will be the methods you will use** and the outcome will be the same until she either submits or leaves home.*

Leslie, some children submit more easily than others. Some learn to "wag their tails" at an early age. They pay a terrible price as adults for this subservience because they must always search for someone or something to control them. They spend their lives searching for someone or something to tell them what is right and, even, what is real. They often go from one idol to another, finding each one, in turn, has feet of clay because, after all, who can tell them they have chosen the perfect idol? They live their lives with the consequence of one decision they made when they submitted to control. As the novelist and philosopher Ayn Rand put it, "At the crossroads of choice between 'I know' and 'they say,' [that person] chose the authority of others."

But Sally has not submitted, and it is for this reason that she still battles against you. It is my job to convince you that this is good, not bad. More important, you can help her change her view of the world. Now it is a place in which she has to battle to maintain control over her behavior. By changing your view of parenting as an exercise in controlling her behavior, you will allow her to make her own decisions and to take responsibility for them.

Leslie's life seemed to revolve around her daughter, Sally. As a single parent with an only child, Leslie tended to treat Sally as her life's work, and found it very difficult to keep any objectivity. She was determined that Sally should not make the mistakes which she had made, her early sexual experimentation, her poor grades, her constant quarreling with her own mother, and, finally, her early and disastrous marriage. Unfortunately, the only model of child rearing she knew was her mother's inept, hysterical attempts. Under stress, it's these early-learned patterns that regulate our parenting behavior, even though we may now know better.

Leslie assumes that her job as a parent requires her to control Sally's behavior. Given that she thinks control is necessary and that control naturally requires threats, she does what comes naturally.

So that Leslie can make sure Sally's life is different from her own, she must ensure that Sally does things differently than Leslie did while growing up. To "make sure" of something requires control. Control of Sally's behavior requires that Sally be made uncomfortable when she does anything that frightens her mother. Control works well with people who are easily intimidated. Sally isn't that kind of person.

Sally retaliates using Leslie's most vulnerable spot. Her mother becomes hysterical and goes too far when provoked by Sally's behavior. These extreme reactions—"You're grounded for life!" or "I give up. You're out of here." —are always rescinded later.

In the next chapter we will watch Leslie learn an alternative way of influencing Sally. The alternative response below previews that approach.

During Sally's junior year she presented Leslie with a "perfect" first-quarter report card of five D's, and, after dinner, asked her mother to sign it.

Leslie's Response

Leslie's first reaction was disbelief: "Are those A's? No, they're D's, every rotten one of them!"

Leslie's own report cards flashed by, scene after scene, of her mother screaming at her, battering her with dire predictions. It was too much! She burst into tears.

Finally, she sobbed out, "I give up. I keep telling you you're wasting your life, but you won't listen! You really don't care, do you?"

Sally: "Why do you care? You're always telling me I'm going to be on welfare."

Leslie: "My feelings don't count for anything. No they don't! After all I've tried to do for you, these are the thanks I get."

Sally: "Maybe if I had a mother who wasn't a High School dropout, I'd have better grades."

Leslie: "You're trying to hurt me on purpose, just to spite

Alternative Response

(Leslie thinks: "My God! How could this happen? She's too bright for this. She must have arranged it. I wonder why?")

Leslie signs the card without comment.

Sally: "Aren't you going to say anything?"

Leslie: "What's to say?"

Sally: "But my grades are pretty bad."

Leslie: "Sally, your grades are your business. Looks to me like something's wrong, but I don't know what it is. It's between you and your teachers."

Sally: "But why should I get good grades? What's the difference?"

Leslie: "Oh well, I know something about that. You said you'd like to go to Antioch or Berkeley or Michigan. They won't accept you with grades like this. Admission is based half on your grades and half on your aptitude scores. You have high aptitude, but a D average will wash you out."

me. That's what you are, a hateful little monster."

Sally: "Oh!"

Sally's grades rose steadily to A's by the end of the year as she realized they were hers and hers alone to worry about. She really wanted to go to a good school. Maybe it was too late, but it was worth a try. And it was kind of fun. Getting good grades turned into a game for her.

Chapter 6

Parenting Using Rules

The therapist had promised Leslie he would help her with her parenting. But so far, the therapist has only worked with her on her expressions of anger and has told her that she doesn't need to try to control her daughter Sally.

One alternative to control struggles with children is parenting using rules. But this alternative is ineffective if Leslie is miserable and angry with Sally. Rule making and rule enforcement simply become gambits in the control struggles between parent and child if the parent remains in the grip of the anger habit. The discussion of the use of rules has awaited Leslie's ability to view her anger and misery as failed attempts to control Sally. The alternative to such control is child management, the establishment and enforcement of rules.

"Rules" are not to be viewed as laws to be obeyed. Rather, they are limits on behavior that the parent promises the child will be noted and responded to consistently. Children are expected to break or "test" rules. The rule is at once a statement of a parent's expectation of how a child should behave and a guarantee of how the parent will respond if the child does not behave that way. The consequence of rule testing should be parental restatement of the rule, not punishment.

When Sally came home after midnight, she broke the rule, "You shall be home by twelve." Non-punitive enforcement of the rule consists of the statement, "You shall be home by midnight."

Leslie, like hundreds of other counseling clients, responds initially to this restatement by asking: "You mean I'm supposed to just let her get away with it?"

As parents' own anger is better understood by them, the answer to this question becomes clearer to them. First, the child has already "gotten away with it" when he or she breaks the rule, if what is meant is that the child is in charge of his or her behavior. The alternative to the child being in control of his or her own behavior is parent's control. Control of children involves attack or threats of an attack, which cannot be avoided by the child. Control is only effective as long as the parent is better at making threats than the child. Both Leslie and Sally are good at avoiding the other's control; so neither is master of the other.

The goal of rule enforcement is not control of the child. The goal is effective parental influence in a safe environment.

The therapist writes a letter to Leslie concerning her need to control Sally.

Dear Leslie:

We have seen that your "blow-ups" at Sally are actually a natural outcome of your belief that you must control your daughter rather than just influence her. You've been taught in a hundred ways that control is your job as a parent. You've been doing it the best you can; that is, you have been trying to establish a more commanding position with respect to Sally from which you can make threats she cannot escape. In short, you have seen parenting as a process of making your child submit to your direction. But Sally does not submit; she fights back.

As you began to see your unhappiness about Sally as part of your attempt to control her, you have been able to let go of your negative attitude. You told me that you feel a big weight has been lifted from you and that you are seeing Sally as less integral to your own happiness. This distancing between your happiness and Sally's behavior has been a big relief to you.

Now, I'm going to show you another way to look at your parenting role. Your job is indeed to influence your child, but not by control. Rather, your role as a parent is, first, to show your child how to behave; and, second, to make sure that she knows what you expect of her. To show Sally how to behave means that every interaction you have with her is a model from which she learns what influences her behavior and the behavior of others. In other words, children do as we do, not as we say.

It is an old concept in psychology that, as adults, we take into ourselves the ways we were talked to and treated as children. This process has been called by several names—"socialization," "introjection," "the formation of conscience," and "modeling." All of these concepts capture a very simple core idea: Children learn about their behavior and the behavior of others from their parents and those around them. It is this "knowledge"—correctly or not—that children then use to influence other's behavior (social interaction), as well as their own (volitional behavior). We are all psychologists and must be so that we can have a conscious influence on the behaviors of others and ourselves. So it seems that our parents and other significant adults are our psychology professors.

When we bring up our children with parenting which primarily emphasizes control, we are teaching them that the way to influence behavior is to gain a threatening position over the person to be managed. They also learn that one must be either in a superior position (have the advantage) or an inferior position (be submissive). When it comes to self-management, these exact same choices apply. The choice is to indulge in our wishes or to submit to our guilty feelings. In your life, Leslie, a major path to a superior position over another person has been to be more distressed than they are. The one who is most unhappy got to control the other in this situation. In this case submission means to "give in" to the other person's claims that you have made them unhappy, and not to do such and such, which "makes" them suffer.

What is an alternative role for you as a parent other than that of control of Sally by being unhappy with her? Because you are teaching Sally how to influence behavior, why not take the teaching role seriously? To do this, you must have some goals and use them in your interactions with Sally, such as...

*1. Children do not know what behaviors to expect from themselves or others in everyday life until they are taught or experience these behaviors. A major influence on their behavior is the parents' persistent expectation about what children will or will not do. **Parents must have expectations and must persist in them.***

2. *Because the child's first two years are dominated by attempted control over his or her parents' behavior through attack (crying, displays of distress, temper tantrums),* **the child must be taught not to use others or be used by them.** *In this way the child may avoid some major sources of distress in his or her life.*

The first of these goals implies that Sally doesn't know a lot about what she is going to do, day in and day out. It is important for her to know what you expect her to do. I'm not talking about a kind of "sneaky control" meaning of "expect" as in "I expected better from you," said in an angry, threatening way. I mean an expectation that expresses real conviction. In other words, a real prediction about Sally's behavior that persists through any short-term indication that it might be wrong.

Leslie, we have many expectations (predictions) about our children's behavior that are communicated without any attempt to make them explicit. Taking your child to school says you expect her to learn. Buying an encyclopedia says she can learn to do research in it. But at the very tip of the iceberg, made up of hundreds of not very clearly communicated expectations, are a few which are and must be clearly communicated. These are called rules.

It is the clarity of rules (expectations about behavior) and, equally important, the persistence with which you are seen by Sally to maintain these rules, that forms the whole basis of your credibility as a source of information for her about what she can expect from herself. When you say to Sally, "You must not date on school nights," you are really saying, "I expect you not to go out on dates on school nights." When she breaks this rule or attempts to do so by getting special permission, you demonstrate your expectation that, in the end, she will not date on school nights by saying "no" or by enforcing the rule (by restatement) if she breaks it.

I must emphasize to you that rules are important for Sally because they give you credibility as a source of expectations about her behavior that she needs from you. Your expectations constitute a kind of ideal picture of Sally, the ways in which she will grow, despite temporary lapses or rule tests.

These rules are not control attempts. They are credibility builders.

When you make a rule for Sally, you are not attempting to take control of her behavior away from her. This would require punishing her if she breaks the rule, which in turn would require that you avoid Sally's ability to punish you for punishing her. As a rule enforcer, you are in the position of a good teacher who expects a student to learn a lesson and perform an assignment correctly. If the student hands the assignment in with incorrect or incomplete work, the teacher will hand it back, still with the expectation that it will be corrected and completed. Handing it back is not an attempt to control. The student can actually continue to turn in sloppy or incomplete work. But, the teacher will also hand the work back to the student until it is satisfactory. The teacher will not settle for less than what she or he expects from the student. The teacher is acting on a conviction that the child can and will do the work, and is communicating this expectation to the child. Once the child does in fact do the assignment properly, the teacher becomes a more credible source of information to the child about what can be expected from oneself.

Rule enforcement with Sally is just like giving her back an incomplete assignment. Your job is not to punish Sally for breaking rules. It is to persist in your expectation that she will behave in the way the rule specifies. This implies, among other things, that effective rule enforcement must be the responsibility of the rule maker. If you are going to enforce someone else's rule (prediction), you had better make it clear to Sally beforehand that you agree with that rule.

So, Leslie, a major alternative to trying to control Sally is to help her "connect up" her behavior to an expectation of what it will be. A major part of being able to plan what we do is the belief that our behaviors will conform to our own expectations. This means that **we must learn to persist in our expectations of our own behaviors**. We will not go further into this connection, but I will say in passing that this connection is necessary for rational behavior. This means that until we learn to persist in our expectations of ourselves, as expressed by our plans, we cannot act rationally. Using reason to decide what to do is useless unless we do it.

*The second goal I mentioned for parenting is to teach Sally not to use or be used by other's emotional displays. Sally must learn that screaming and yelling and pouting and freezing others out are ways of behaving that make **her** miserable. There are more effective ways to get what she wants than by making herself miserable in an effort to make others miserable.*

*How to teach Sally **not** to use anger to get what she wants is for you to avoid letting her anger "use" you. When you enforce rules that Sally has broken, you are always to enforce them the same way and not respond to her anger in any way. If Sally breaks a rule for the third time, your response must be the same as it was the first time she broke the rule. The easiest way to make your enforcement consistent is to restate the rule is an unemotional way.*

In not allowing Sally's anger to change your behavior toward her, you are not only refusing to let her use you, but you are showing her that she need not respond to other's attacks. You are teaching her by providing no reward for her anger displays; and you are providing a model for her, yourself, of someone who persists in goals without being manipulated by the anger of others.

*Now, let's look at the differences between approaching your role as a parent, as a teacher, and as a model, as opposed to a controlling authority. As a controller of Sally, you must do what any controller must do. You must establish a superior position from which you can issue threats without being vulnerable to Sally's attempts to counter them. This means you are always seeking more power over her—ways to punish or authorities to call on at school or in the courts, or her father, or a counselor to augment your position in order to **make her** behave. You might seek ways to make Sally see your misery with her and that your misery is greater than hers is with you. This is continually frustrating and you find yourself to be continually angry, or at least living with a very short fuse. You also continually feel guilty. You are concerned about the excesses, which accompany your anger. You look on yourself as a bad mother. You try to rescue yourself from this guilt by seeing your daughter as especially bad or mentally ill. But this rescue never works for long because you realize that there still must be something you should be doing. And you always end by becoming angry with Sally when you try to impose control.*

You, as Sally's teacher, must give up on your goal of control. Sally's behavior is under her own control and always has been and always will be. Your job as her teacher is to provide expectations for her behavior (rules) and to persist in those expectations. Your job is also to keep her from using you with her anger. This would have been impossible for you to do before you recognized that your misery and anger were your desperate attempt to control Sally. But, now that you have laid claim to your own happiness and are viewing Sally as a separate person who is under her own control, it is achievable.

*I'm not asking you to do anything that isn't possible for you. You don't have to **make her** do anything. **It's all your behavior and under your control**. It will be hard to stand up to her screaming and persist in merely saying, "You must go to school." It may mean missing an appointment some morning while you wait her out. But, it's still under your control to do it.*

And now, here's the good part. Leslie, homes do not have to be filled with tension, anger, and emotional outbursts during the child-rearing years. They tend to be that way for only one reason: The attempts of all concerned to establish control over others in the family, which inevitably means displays of anger and distress on everyone's part. When you change that in your parenting of Sally, she will calm down and so will you. You will find that parenting can be a delight rather than a burden.

As you establish yourself as a source of authority concerning information for Sally, rather than as an authority in control of her, you and she will be able to talk, to laugh, and to enjoy her growing up. This is the light at the end of the tunnel, of your trying to do what I'm asking you to do. This will be your reward for doing the hard, but doable task of rule enforcement.

A Leslie-Sally Success Story

Sally: "Mother, Janie is having this big party at her house next Thursday and I have to go."

Old Behaviors	Leslie's Response
Leslie: "Now, you know we agreed that you wouldn't go out on school nights." *Sally*: "But, Mom, this is different! It's Jeff Lee's birthday. You know, the football star and all the players will be there, and it's going to be a really big bash. All the really *in* girls are going to be there and I was specially invited. Even Jeff asked if I'd be there. And I can wear my new slinky outfit." *Leslie*: "There's going to be a lot of other parties. It won't hurt you to miss this one." *Sally* (in tears): "Mom, you're so conservative! You don't want me to have any fun! All my friends are going, even Sophie, and you know how mean her parents are. C'mon, mom, I'll even do the dishes for a whole month. And I promise not to swear anymore. Just this once? Please, please? Please!" *Leslie*: Oh, all right! But just this once!"	*Leslie*: "You may not go out on school nights." *Sally*: "But Mom, this is different. It's Jeff Lee's birthday, the football star, and all the players are going to be there, and it's going to be a really big bash. All the really *in* girls are going to be there and I was specially invited. Even Jeff asked if I'd be there. And I can wear my new slinky outfit." *Leslie*: "You may not go out on school nights." *Sally* (in tears): "Mom, you're so conservative! You never let me go anywhere! You don't want me to have any fun! All my friends are going, even Sophie, and you know how mean her parents are. C'mon, mom, I'll even do the dishes for a whole month. And I won't swear any more. Just this once? Please, Please? Please!" *Leslie*: "You may not go out on school nights."

When a person is being held responsible for the well being of another, that person may be said to be in authority over the other. Parents are in authority over their children. The appropriate management technique for those in authority is rule enforcement.

When two people interact and neither is accountable for the well-being of the other, neither one is in authority. Co-workers are not answerable for each other's behavior. The appropriate management technique for co-workers is information feedback on emotional responses ("It upsets me when you..."). Chapter 10 provides further discussion on this kind of voluntary interaction.

When Management Is Appropriate

One in Authority *Persistent Rules*	Neither in Authority *Voluntary Interaction*
Parent-Child	Worker-Worker
Employer-Employee	Spouse-Spouse
Teacher-Student	Neighbor-Neighbor
Judge-Criminal	Sibling-Sibling
Internal Revenue Service-Citizen	Citizen-Citizen

While we are taken over by anger, it is difficult to see that each of us has control of our own behaviors. We become so intent on controlling other people's behavior that we lose the sense of what is in our control and what is not. Influence on other's behaviors for whom we are responsible is well within our capability, just as Leslie can and is learning to influence Sally. But others' behavior is still their own and so, in the words of the song,

"You don't always get what you want." But you can **do** what you want. So why not concentrate on what you **can** do that will stand some chance of producing what you want?

Making clear what we expect from others is a way of influencing what they do. Maintaining that expectation in the face of "failures" on their part is a powerful force for change in them. And it is entirely within our control.

Chapter 7

Parenting With Reason

The stories about Rick and Leslie show us what attempts to control can do to relationships. The long-term consequences of growing up in an atmosphere of control to Rick and the ravages on Leslie and her daughter Sally of conflict stemming from attempts to control are clear and overwhelming.

An alternative to control, the concept of rational parenting, requires the persistent enforcement of rules. Since parenting is the prototype of all potentially dominant-submissive relationships, other examples including some outside the home, appear in this chapter.

Non-angry parents recognize anger in a child and identify it as "a child in distress." The parents don't take the anger personally. They analyze the problem and take corrective action when it is appropriate. Sometimes, no action should be taken; for example, when the anger results from a child's wrong prediction such as when a child throws a temper tantrum over a birthday present.

An infant or child in pain acts angry and may then receive attention. But the parents may overlook the pain signal and focus on the yelling, crying, and screaming as attacks on them. They may take the anger personally. These parents may treat the child's anger as an attempt to control them. The parent then responds angrily by counterattacking; and frightens the child, who either submits or sends out further distress signals by "fighting back." If the child fights back, what began as a request for help turns into a confrontation, with both sides acting like angry two-year-olds. Each side sends out distress calls, which are misinterpreted as attempts to dominate or control the other.

But when parents recognize a child's anger as a response to distress and a signal that the child may need help, parents do not become angry. They may be able to do something rational like reducing the pain, comforting the child, feeding the child, looking for signs of ear infection, or rubbing the child's gums. In short, they can do some parenting.

Awareness of our own fear and anger is important information. But we must be clear what this awareness means. Awareness of fear **does not** mean awareness of danger. We may **think** there is danger when we **feel** fear. But awareness of fear is awareness of one's body preparing to **deal with** danger. When a sudden noise frightens you, it is your rapid heart rate, tingling on the back of your neck, and other body sensations which you feel as fear even before you are able to look around and see what has happened.

Similarly, awareness of anger **does not** mean awareness of an enemy. We may **think** we have an enemy when we **feel** anger. But awareness of anger, like fear, is awareness of our preparation to deal with an adversary. To be aware of anger means to be aware we are preparing to attack, are analyzing the potential sources of counterattack and our vulnerable points. Fear and anger are automatic responses. And they are natural. But our **awareness** of our fear and anger gives us an opportunity to review the situation and choose what to do.

We can "do what comes naturally" which usually means being controlled by blind emotion, "acting like a two-year-old," acting without thinking.

We can "act rationally" which means analyzing the situation, explaining it to ourselves with words, and acting humanely. It means allowing ourselves time to empathize and to care about what another person is feeling:

—With an infant. Is the baby hurting?

—With a child. Is the child hurting?

—With a friend. Is the person hurting?

—With a spouse. Is the wife or husband hurting?

—With an employee. Is the worker hurting?

Irrational behavior, acting under the direction of blind emotion, is appropriate for infants. Rational behavior, acting under the influence of knowledge and empathy, is appropriate for older children and adults.

Good parenting behaviors are actions resulting from rational decisions. Rational decisions about parenting result from predictions tested by our experience. The relevant predictions are those influenced by empathy; for example, if I do this, the person will feel better. Empathy is the recognition of our own emotional responses occurring in others whom we care about. We might think—when I acted like that, I was feeling like this. Good parenting includes persistence in pursuing a reasoned course of action despite short-term increases in emotionality.

Difficult child behavior is not terribly rare or unusual. Charlie and Anne thought of themselves as good parents, but somehow they had produced a child monster! Just look at Chuckie's room, they told each other. Chuckie was only three years old and he's torn the wallpaper, broken a lamp, left big gouges in the headboard of the bed by hitting it with his truck, broken or battered almost every one of his toys, and spilled finger paints on the rug and window shade! And now he was beginning to take his anger out on the new baby. Charlie and Anne had to watch him every minute!

As they examined the mess, a baby's shriek shattered the silence. Charlie and Anne rushed into the nursery. The bassinet was tipped over and the baby was on the floor. Chuckie was standing over her with a mean look on his face.

Charlie's Response Choices

Charlie's Response

Charlie: "You little monster! What have you done! Boy, you've pushed me too far this time! You're going to get the beating of your life!"

(Charlie thought, "He's really sick! I've got to do something. The next time he'll kill her. I've got to stop him somehow—beat the daylights out of him!")

Charlie grabbed Chuckie by the arm and slammed his open hand across the boy's face, again and again.

Anne screamed: "No, Charles, No!"

Charlie then took Chuckie by his collar and dragged him through the hall to the boy's room. Charlie slid off his leather belt and beat the boy across the back and buttocks. Throughout this ordeal, Chuckie made not a sound. Finally, his father threw him on the bed and left.

Alternative Response

(Charlie thought: "That little monster!")

Charlie: "Anne! Check the baby!"

(Charlie thought: "He had to do that. Why did he have to do that? I don't know, but he has to see the damage he's done!")

Charlie walked Chuckie over to witness Anne's examination of the baby. There was a lump on the baby's forehead. Anne applied a cold compress to the lump and held the baby, crooning to her.

Charlie walked the boy to his room and said: "We do not hurt the baby. You stay here until you feel better."

Nothing further was said about the incident. Charlie and Anne agreed that Chuckie would not be left alone with the baby until he had developed control of his impulses.

Rational decisions do not occur when we are angry or fearful. It is necessary to recognize our fear and our anger and, if possible, to wait until the emotion subsides in order to avoid making irrational decisions.

As children begin to develop language, they become aware that they can sometimes use anger to control their parents' behavior toward them. And, if children are sometimes successful at these first manipulations, it's a small learning step to discover that they can speed up slow-moving parents by intensifying their screams. This is how "brat" behavior is trained into children by parents.

Good parenting requires that we determine the reason for the child's pain before acting to relieve it. If the reason for the pain is an unfulfilled prediction, rather than a physical hurt, then parents must think twice before taking action.

For example, when two-year-old Jeanie's father returned from a trip, he gave Jeanie a small package of peanuts he had picked up on the plane. The next time he returned from a trip, Jeanie waited with an expectant look. The father said, "No, Jeanie, I didn't bring peanuts." Jeanie had a temper tantrum. Due to her limited experience, she had learned that "daddy comes home, and I get peanuts." She was operating under the control of an "accidental contingency" or connection.

Jeanie's father thought, "Do I have to pick up a gift to avoid a scene like that? No, of course not. Jeanie's prediction was reasonable in light of her experience, but my gift-giving is unpredictable. I give gifts when the spirit moves me, not because someone expects them. With one or two more tantrums, she'll learn not to use my gift-giving to reduce her tension. She'll learn not to expect a gift each time."

Jeanie's anger was appropriate in light of her earlier learning. And she was in pain. But the prediction of her father's behavior was based on a single event. Her unfulfilled prediction was her problem, not her father's problem. He must be careful not to change his behavior in order to fit her "superstition" behavior, which is behavior resulting from an accidental contingency or connection.

In like manner, parents must be careful to avoid being manipulated by children. The analytic thinking required to avoid the manipulation trap requires that parents not respond, either fearfully or angrily, to a child's anger.

An important part of parenting amounts to avoiding control struggles with our children. We can do this by not being controlled by any behavior of theirs that has as its object the control of our behavior through threat or attack. We are able to avoid struggles with children when we respond to attacks, first, by interpreting attacks as distress signals, and, second, by determining what it is best to do. We must not change our behavior either to fulfill inappropriate expectations (predictions) of others, or to avoid making others angry. Their anger is, after all, their problem, not ours.

To summarize, in the case of accidental contingencies, anger caused by unfulfilled predictions provides its own corrective. The anger is the problem of the angry person and should receive no response from the person at whom the anger is directed. If the angry behavior results in a change in the caregiver's behavior, then the child's anger may be used to manipulate that behavior in the future.

The avoidance of control struggles with children can be achieved by persisting in expectations and the refusal to be manipulated by angry displays and attacks.

This is also true in typical manager-employee situations:

A Management Scene

Steve was a graduate student working in a school service unit, helping younger students succeed in college. He knocked on the director's door and said, "Got a minute? I have to talk with you."

Director: "C'mon in."

Steve: "I mean I've really got to get some things off my chest. I'm damn mad about what's happening around here!"

Director: "Hm-m-m."

Steve: "I don't like what's happening. I don't like what you're doing to me or the staff. I mean, half of them aren't pulling their weight…and you aren't doing anything about it. And it's not fair! It's not fair to me or to them. And you just sit here like a damn mogul and let it happen!"

Director's Response Choices

Director's Response

Director: "You're telling me I'm incompetent? My God, you've got a lot of gall! Get the hell out of here and get back to work! If you've got a grievance, go make out the papers! Better yet, go find a job elsewhere. I'm tired of your goddamn grousing."

Alternative Response

Director: "You mean I don't do enough directing."

Steve: "You're damn right. You never criticize people. You haven't fired anybody since I've been here. All you ever do is comment on what they're doing right. It's like you're afraid to bawl them out. And they all think you're a prince. And it's not true! What you are is a lousy director with no guts! "

Director: "Uh-huh. Anything else?"

Steve: "Uh-h…no. I guess that's it. Well, I guess I'll go back to work."

Director: "OK. Any time."

While the feeling of anger is originally associated with pain, it soon comes to be aroused whenever a predicted event fails to occur. Some form of discomfort or distress is an essential part of any learning process. The behaviors that follow the distress, called the "display," are influenced by the subsequent behavior of the object of the anger. Such displays are often interpreted by others as demands on them and arouse anger followed by others' attempts to control the person who began the cycle.

In this way each generation trains its children in the anger habit and in the struggle for control. Rational parenting includes recognition of the child's feelings and rational care taking without either being controlled by the child's anger or attempting to counter it. The child, after all, will take these feelings and the learning into the adult world.

Anger, in those for whom we are responsible, is trained and perfected by our own angry responses. Consistent rational responses to the distress of children and others for whom we are responsible produce creative solutions to real problems and adds the benefit of not rewarding manipulative emotional displays.

Chapter 8

Communicating Without Effect

When we struggle for control with others we must hide our weaknesses, or they will be used against us. One of the outcomes of habitual struggle with others is to always conceal things from them. This is a tremendous strain.

In Chapter 8 we will examine the price to be paid for a family control struggle and its attendant secretiveness, which brings about an alienated teenager.

Dear Mark:

When your mother first brought you to me, she was very concerned about you. She said you were getting into a lot of trouble in the eighth grade, fighting and breaking rules and earning low grades. She also said that you didn't obey her at home, and you sometimes got terribly angry, even threatening to hurt her.

What had her most concerned though, Mark, was that you had been talking to her about hurting yourself. And this was also scaring you and originally made you willing to come in.

Mark we've come a long way together in understanding what was going on in your life then. I want to review with you some of the accomplishments you've achieved and talk about what I'd like you to work on next.

When you first came here, Mark, you were terribly angry and frightened. Remember how you used to describe yourself as feeling like you were going to explode? At the same time, you felt isolated from others and as if you didn't belong anywhere on this earth, except in your own room at home, alone. Remember my using the word "alienated"? You asked me what it meant? I told you it meant you felt like an alien, like someone from another planet; and you lit up and said that's exactly right.

We talked about how you had gotten to feel that way. I told you these feelings came from some very good reasons and that these reasons had nothing to do with your being defective, or sick, or different from other people. I explained that you felt as if you didn't belong anywhere because you didn't feel that your behavior belonged to you, in school or at home or around just about anyone, except with one or two people whom you saw as being as odd as you.

We spent a long time talking about how this came about and how it's a problem for an awful lot of people. I explained how your mother and school teachers do a lot of things they say are in your interest, but these actions are actually in their own interest. It is important, I said, for you to see and understand this. Most of these things have to do with control. When your teacher or your mother gets angry, it is just a temper tantrum because they aren't getting their way. That's their problem, not yours. Even more important, you started to see the same was true of your own behavior. Your anger was your temper-tantrum-self trying to get its way; and it was your problem, not your mother's or your teacher's.

As you began to see the importance of control to so many people, you also began to see how much of your life was a struggle against control by others. Whether it's on the playground arguing over whose turn it was to bat, or at home arguing about cleaning up your room, the people around you were struggling to control others by attacking or preparing to attack by getting their defenses ready.

Then, Mark, you discovered something very peculiar about struggling against control. When you thought you were resisting others—your mother or teachers or some kid on the playground—by striking out, or swearing, or attacking them, or not doing your work, or doing it poorly, when you refused to submit by fighting back in these ways, you were just as much controlled by them as if you had submitted to begin with. When your teacher told you to sit down, it didn't matter whether you sat or called her "bitch," the behavior still didn't feel like your own. You felt as if you were controlled, used and abused, by the teacher.

When your mother told you to clean your room, it didn't matter whether you did it or argued with her, you still couldn't feel as if you were doing what **you** had decided to do.

You began to see, Mark, that the only part of you, which you could call your own, was your extremely private thoughts and secret behaviors. Your sexual fantasies and angry thoughts felt as if they were yours. The sneaky behaviors of cheating and stealing and disturbing other peoples' property without their knowing it felt like your behavior.

But these secret thoughts and behaviors were mostly unacceptable things. They were what you had to keep secret or other people would get very upset with you. In other words, people would attack and reject you, and maybe even drive you further away from them. Worst of all, you would lose even more of what little there was of you.

Things started to change for you, Mark, when two things happened. The first was that you began to trust me when I told you I wasn't going to attack you or be disgusted with you about your thoughts and actions. You began to see that I wasn't trying to control you. I'm trying to help you understand what is happening in your life, and I firmly believe and expect that you will change and be happier when you learn more about yourself and others. You did a lot of things to try to provoke me to see if I would attack you. You spilled my coffee. You lied to your mother about your appointments and did not show up. You even made a show out of farting into my wastebasket with my college's name on it to show your disgust with my education.

But gradually you saw that I wasn't interested in engaging in a struggle with you to control your behavior. You saw that I am just as interested in your behavior being under your control as you are, and in a way, even more so because I really believe it can and will be the case.

The second thing that happened, which helped things change for you, was that your mother started being more consistent with you and less angry. At my urging she became stricter with you. She didn't tell you to do something and *then go away and yell at you later for not doing it. Rather, when she told you to do something, she stayed around until it was done. She began to see that you didn't need her to control your behavior. What you needed from her were some expectations on her part about your behavior, expectations that she does not change from moment to moment or day to day. So, yes, you will make your bed in the morning; and, yes, you will do your homework. Your mother has stopped attacking you when you slip up, but she goes right on expecting that you will do these things and showing you that she expects you to do them.*

So, Mark, you now find that more and more of your behavior seems like yours, as if it was you who decided to act in a certain way. If you don't do your homework you know that your mother will ask to see it and she will then tell you to do it. But you also know that that is all she will do. She will not punish you. She will not get "all bent out of shape." She will just tell you to do your homework. And if you mess up and get into trouble at school, she will talk to you and try to find out why that happened. She will not like it and she may tell you so. But that's all she will do. She will not attack you and try to hurt you and make you into some kind of reject. Your behavior now belongs to you, Mark. You may run into some teachers and others who threaten you with disapproval and get angry with you. But, more and more, you see them as just people having temper tantrums in order to get their own way. Remember how you responded to your Pony League coach when he blew his top at you for deciding not to sign up to play last summer? He shouted at you and said you had a "bad attitude" and got very irate with you. You laughed when you told me about the incident and said that he acted like a two-year-old. And you were exactly right. Maybe you did blow it. Maybe you would have been another Babe Ruth of baseball. But it was your decision to make and you made it; and you will be the one to live with it. Personally I think you made the right choice. That was the summer you got involved with playing the guitar and you are getting a lot of enjoyment out of that and working hard at it.

You have learned that there are many things you might do which would upset your mother or other people. It is you who must decide whether to do these things. But there's a big difference between not doing something because it would cause distress to someone you care about, and not doing something so that someone will stop using their distress to control you. To be concerned with someone's distress is to care about him or her. To allow someone to manipulate you by displaying anger or contempt toward you is to be used by him or her.

The fact is, Mark, you care very much about your mother. You are finding that the less you two respond to each other's anger, the more caring there is between you. In other words, the less each of you allow yourselves to be used by the other one, the easier it is to get along.

And now, Mark, where do we go from here? You still have a lot of school problems. Your grades aren't failing grades, but they aren't anything like what you really would like them to be. You sit down to study, but most of the time you don't do a very thorough job of it. You end up "winging it" on tests and preparing assignments at the last minute. You know me well enough by now to realize that I'm not attacking you when I say these things. This is just the way your behavior is. What I'd like to have you do is to understand why this comes about, so you can see a way to change the behavior if you want to.

Ever since you've been in school, Mark, you've been told that you have great potential, and you should be doing much better than you are. The problem is that it scares the dickens out of you to put it to the test. Can you do better or not? You have what some psychologists call a "high fear of failure."

That sounds funny, doesn't it? How could you be afraid of failure? You're used to failing tests you don't study for. But you know and I know that's not really failing. After all, how is it a failure to not pass a test you didn't study for? Who would expect you to do well on the test if you weren't prepared? A lot of the time you do okay anyway, and sometimes you actually ace those tests. That really shows how much you could do if you only applied yourself. So you're in a no-risk situation if you don't really study. You can't fail if you don't try; and you might do well anyway, which would show how bright you actually are and how much potential you really have.

Now comes the big question. What's so scary about failure? What are you risking if you were actually to do some minimal studying and then didn't do great on a test? What if you actually put some time and effort into an assignment and then got a C?

We've talked a lot about anger, Mark, yours and other people's. Now I'm going to ask you to look at your anger and your struggle to control it. What I want you to see is that your fear of failure, the risk you take when you put forth real effort, is really just your awareness of your vulnerability if you were to attack other people. Controlling others means having an advantage over them. In order to get your mother off your back by stopping her from talking to you about your friends or your grades or your father or whatever, even if she wants to continue talking, you must be able to threaten her with something in such a way that you can carry out the threat and she can't do a thing about it. That is the nature of control over others; they must take it whether they like it or not. So you must be in a superior position. You must be able to threaten without being vulnerable yourself. This means that, to the extent that you engage in struggles with others to make them stop a specific behavior, to that extent you must be invulnerable. The more you make it your business to check out what your teachers do, the more risky it will be for you to take a chance on studying. The more you take personally what other students say and do, the more scary it will be for you to risk exposing anything of yourself.

Mark, it's as simple as this: If you're going to fight with others, you're going to need armor. If you can bring yourself to see that you don't need to fight with them, then you don't need to prepare for fighting. If you don't need to prepare for fighting, you don't need to protect your weakness from discovery by others.

The behavior you need to perform in order to get higher grades is your business, Mark. Nobody else's. If somebody else makes it their business, they either care about you and are just making a mistake about how to do it, or they are just trying to pick a fight. It's up to you to decide whether you want to fight with every busybody who comes along or not. If you do, you will have to be a busybody, too, because you will have to determine what their judgments of you are, and then make it your business to modify their judgments.

So, Mark, this is what I'd like you to work on. I want you to start looking at teachers' interactions with you and with other students for evidence of *whether teachers are minding their own business or whether they're being busy-bodies. You already know a lot about making this distinction, but you don't know that you know it. For instance, remember the other day you told me that the principal came up to you and shook your hand vigorously and patted you on the back saying how happy she was that you hadn't gotten into trouble for a long time? You told me that when this happened, you thought it was weird and that the principal is strange. I asked you if you thought she was really as happy about your record as she was saying, and you said no. Well, Mark, she was being a busybody and you recognized it, only you didn't call it that. What you picked up was that she was acting in a certain way in order to try to have an effect on your future behavior. She was making your behavior her business. So you can count that as your first identification of busybody behavior at school.*

*The next step, Mark, is for you to learn that you don't need to make your teachers' attempts to control—their busybody behaviors—your business. You will not be able to see that you make their behaviors your business until you see their control attempts clearly. When you identify their busybody behavior, you will be in a position to see your response to it in the same way as you responded to your principal when you called her "weird." You will be in a position to do your work and be happy or unhappy with the outcome and others' responses to it. But you will not have to bother with controlling others' judgments of you or your work. You will be able to work **openly** on your grades if you wish, without being concerned about what will be revealed to others. That will simplify your life and make you more comfortable.*

The alternative to control struggles and their attendant secretiveness is communication. Early in Mark's therapy, his mother came across a cache of girlie magazines he had carefully hidden under his mattress.

His mother said, "Dirty, filthy magazines! Where did you get them? Well, where did they come from?"

Control Struggle

Mark: "Jeez, Mom, those are mine. Why do you have to go muckin' around in my room for?"

Mother: "Never mind that! Where did you get them?"

Mark: "I bought 'em."

Mother: "I don't know what I'm going to do with you. This is sick, sick, sick! You're getting more like your Uncle Henry every day. You must be a throwback—perverted, that's what you are. You keep this up and you will rot in jail, just the way he did!"

Mark: "Here we go again. Just like your Uncle Henry—a pervert. Why can't you be good like your big brother?"

Mother: "So, why can't you be good like your big brother?"

Mark: "Jeez, I'm so damn tired of hearing that! Always on my back. So I'm bad. What do you want from your bad son?"

Mother: "Show me some respect young man!"

Mark: (He thinks "I'm going to kill her, I swear, someday I'm going to kill the old bat!") "Leave me alone! Leave me alone, do you hear me! Leave me the hell alone!"

Mother: "Don't you dare talk to me like that, young man!"

Communication

Mark: "Those are mine. I stowed them under my mattress, out of the way, so they wouldn't upset you."

Mother: "Where did you get them?"

Mark: "I bought them. It upsets me when you search my room. Those magazines are my business. Please respect my right to privacy."

Mother: "I was turning your mattress and found them. You're right of course. They are your business. I just had a feeling of dread when I saw them. Now that I think about it, I think my feeling was connected with my brother."

Mark: "You mean weird old Uncle Henry?"

Mother: "Yes. But you're nothing like him, thank heavens!"

She hands Mark his magazines.

Alienation, the feeling and behavior of one who does not belong to the community, results from the inability to exchange information honestly. In close relationships of family and friends, alienation destroys intimacy. Intimacy necessarily involves the revealing of information, which **could** be used to hurt. This is because trust is required before intimate feelings can occur. In fact, we even **use** revelation of our secrets to establish or test friendship. By the time we are in the third grade we may have experienced a friendship based on mutual sharing of secrets.

Communication is nearly impossible between and among people when they are struggling to control others and to keep from being controlled because the information they exchange is constantly being sorted for clues of attacks. As bad as this is for communication, it is even worse for intimacy, which **requires** making oneself vulnerable.

Mark's feelings of alienation were caused by his control struggles with those around him. These struggles resulted in interactions that were typically dominated by jockeying for positions from which he could control others while being invulnerable to effective counterattacks. His adult caretakers participated with him in this struggle without being able to break out of the lock their mutual struggles for control had on them. This resulted in a quite typical situation where everybody involved was concerned and suffering without being able to talk about the situation or communicate.

The more Mark and his family attempted to "get through," the farther they got from each other. Each attempt to "communicate" was seen by Mark as an attempt to control. He listened for what others wanted him to do, rather than for information about what was what. It had gotten to the point where if his mother remarked on what a nice day it was, Mark would hear her "weather report" as a push for him to rake the yard. The family was experiencing the excruciating result of lost communication due to their use of language to manipulate each other instead of using it to communicate facts and beliefs.

Breaking out from the struggle for control is something each individual must accomplish for himself or herself and always involves learning to ignore some attempts by others to "keep you in the game." In many clinical cases, such as Mark's, this process is aided when other family members are also attempting to cope with **their** control-related problems by examining their struggles for control.

Chapter 9

From Anger to Panic

Mark's alienation problem (see Chapter 8) involved a relatively low level, but chronically present, orientation of being defensive. He felt under attack from control efforts by others and made the situation worse by his efforts at controlling others. Because Mark's efforts resulted in increased countermeasures by these others, and that in turn increased his efforts to control, a vicious circle occurred. This resulted in a more-or-less steady struggle. Because control involves causing discomfort by bringing threats to bear, it necessarily interferes with openness and honesty. Control keeps a person such as Mark from being close to others. As a result Mark was isolated from those he cared most about and they were unable to help him. That was the basis of his alienation.

Now we come to a rather peculiar, but common, result of using threats and dire warnings in order to control. We are all, first and foremost, managers of our behaviors before we can even think of influencing others. What happens when our "self-management technique" is based on emotional displays? We saw in the case of Mark how interpersonal control efforts led to alienation. Can something like alienation occur within ourselves if we try to control ourselves in this manner? What does that mean and what is the result?

In the following case of Marian, and David in Chapter 10, we will explore some of the internal consequences of using anger in the service of **self**-control.

Dear Marian:

You have come to me asking for help, but not really believing there is any such thing. You have periods of feeling so terribly frightened and desperate that all you can do is reach out for anyone available who can to help you to feel calm again. You have told me quite a lot about how you are feeling and what you are going through, and now I'm going to make some guesses about your history.

These problems typically develop over an extended period of time. You have been unhappy with your life. You were unhappy with your husband or parents or children or job or some combination of these. You tried to talk to your husband from time to time about your dissatisfaction, but it always seemed to come out as an attack and resulted in unhappiness for both of you. Your discomfort got worse, and you began to experience emotions you had difficulty accounting for—sadness, when there seemed to be no particular reason to be sad; fear when you were alone.

You probably found a friend or relative or minister or perhaps all of these people, one after another, to talk to. These talks seemed to help a lot at first. You could get your feelings "off your chest," and your friend or whoever seemed to listen and to be sympathetic. With one friend or another you probably talked about your parents and childhood and your unmet needs. You "explored" your feelings about your husband and his bad habits and his criticisms or his weakness or his neglect, whatever fits the situation.

As I said, these talks seemed to help you at first. You had a sympathetic friend. As time went on, though, you seemed always to be covering the same stuff. After a time your friends seemed to get a little less sympathetic and more impatient with you. They began telling you more directly what you should be doing... "You've just got to decide whether to stay in your marriage." Or "I've told you before that you have to be more consistent with your children." Or "You just have to relax; you have nothing to be afraid of."

As your friends got more impatient, you got more uncomfortable and fearful. You felt more than ever that there was something wrong with you to be feeling this way.

It has always seemed to you that you are different from others and apart from them in some way. You may sometimes try to think of this difference as being good. Then you try to reassure yourself that you are more sensitive or more aware than others. It has always seemed to you that life is simpler or easier for other people. They seem to be more in charge of their lives. They seem like adults who are self-assured and competent, while you have always felt like a child, pretending to be an adult.

Others seem to do things to secure pleasure, while you do things to avoid guilt. So when your friend started to get more impatient with you, it frightened or perhaps depressed you even more than before. You felt that this person didn't really understand what was happening to you. The friend was asking you to do things about your life that assumed you were "just like everybody else;" that is, you could just do what makes sense and be happy with it.

But you don't feel that you're like an "ordinary person" who can just see what needs to be done and happily do it. You can't just "control yourself" and "stop bugging your husband" or just "pull yourself together." It's not that easy.

Now you are in an even bigger quandary than before you got some "help." You are feeling even more apart, and your friend seems to be pulling back from you even more and perhaps openly suggesting, "You need help."

You woke up one night and started to experience full-blown panic. You had to get out of bed because you just could not lie still. You paced the floor. You called on someone, anyone, to be with you. All they said was, "You're okay. There is no reason to be afraid." But to you they looked scared themselves. You thought, "I'm going crazy. This is what a nervous breakdown must be." Or "Am I having a heart attack?"

Your friend finally took you to a hospital emergency room. The physician listened to your heart and breathing, took some blood, and perhaps took an EKG. She found no evidence of a heart attack. She told you that you were having an anxiety attack, gave you a shot of the anti-anxiety drug Valium, and sent you home.

This may have been just the beginning of your trips to hospital emergency rooms. Perhaps a friend told you that she heard or read about hypoglycemia (low blood sugar) and that you should have your doctor check this out because it caused symptoms like yours. You mentioned this to your physician, but she brushed it off. So, finally, at the urging of your friend, you went to another physician. He ordered a five hour glucose tolerance test. It showed normal carbohydrate metabolism.

Then you "learned" from someone else that you can't really tell hypoglycemia is causing these symptoms unless a blood sample is taken during an attack.

Sooner or later you came in contact with an emergency room physician or a private physician who sent you to a psychologist or a mental health clinic while you were experiencing a spell of agitation and desperation. At the clinic you were told that you needed to be in a hospital.

As a result your fears that you were crazy or going crazy were confirmed; your anxiety was somewhat relieved because you now thought the professionals at the clinic really knew what to do for you; and your family, friends, and your physician were comforted because you were out of their hair and they could stop worrying about what to do with you.

While you were in the hospital you were given a lot of medications and you slept a lot. You started gaining weight. You hardly ever saw your psychiatrist and, when you did see him if he were from some other country you may not have been able to understand what he said. You saw some kind of counselor every day who talked to you sympathetically and also talked to your relatives. You attended various activities in the hospital and perhaps went to group counseling. You may have been given some projects which "taught you" how to raise your self-esteem or how to be more assertive.

In any case, after a few weeks you were sent home. You still took medication, but you generally felt better. You weren't exactly sure what had happened during the hospital stay, but you thought it must have helped you.

Now, Marian, you are again experiencing anxiety and agitation and some depression. Your relatives look worried about you. You are afraid that what happened before is going to happen again, that you may have to go back to the hospital.

Marian, I went through these guesses about your history to show you that I understand what you're going through. I need you to believe that I understand what's happening to you so that you will trust what I say because I'm going to ask you to do something that is just the opposite of what you've been trying to do up to now.

What I want you to do, Marian, is to stop trying to control your fear. You are afraid that if you don't "keep hold" of your feelings, something terrible will happen. Loss of control means craziness to you. You are not crazy, Marian, and you aren't going to go crazy. What has happened to you is that the more you tried to control your fearful feelings, the more fear you produced.

Let me try to convince you that feelings get more intense when you try to control them. For example, you may have the urge to laugh in a situation where it would be embarrassing to do so. Perhaps once in school, when the teacher was talking very seriously, something struck you as funny. You started to smile and perhaps looked over and saw a friend looking at you, and you immediately saw that your friend felt it funny too. Then the torture started. You tried to keep from laughing aloud. You squirmed, looked down, and covered your face. The more you tried to stifle the laugh, the stronger it got.

Another example is your first visit to my office. You were trying to keep from crying. I said to you, "It's okay to cry. There are tissues there. You can cry and talk at the same time."

Marian, five minutes later there were still no tears. If I had said to you, "Now, stop your crying and get on with it," you would have been stifling your feelings and fighting your tears the whole hour.

Well, fear works the same way. The more you try to control fear, the stronger the feeling of being afraid gets. Now, what I want you to do is very difficult, but you are used to doing very difficult, in fact impossible things, such as controlling your fear. What I'm asking you to do is only difficult; it's not impossible. When you are afraid I want you to do just the opposite from what your instinct dictates. Your instinct is to try to stop feeling afraid. You try to reassure yourself. You tell yourself, "I just can't lose control! " And "Stop it! " And

"There is nothing to fear! " And "If you keep this up, you are going to go over the edge! " And lots of other things.

I'm asking you to do just the opposite. I want you to say to yourself, "Go ahead and come, fear, and do your worst." I want you to submit to the fear just as you might lie on the beach and let waves roll over you.

This is very difficult to learn to do because it runs contrary to your habit of responding by attempting control (in this case, "self-control"). But you can do it, just as you could learn not to flinch if someone shakes a fist in your face. Just because your instinct is to flinch from the fist doesn't mean you must do so. Well, just because you are in the habit of attempting to control your fearful feelings doesn't mean you must do so.

You see, Marian, fear is a body sensation, which you feel when certain chemicals are released into your bloodstream and into your nervous system. The problem is that these chemicals take effect very quickly when released, but their effect takes several minutes to wear off. When you start trying to control the feeling of fear, many of the things you are saying to yourself are threatening things. So, you keep releasing jolts of these chemicals, and never give yourself a chance to have them wear off by themselves.

When you first had a panic attack, the thought entered your mind, "I'm having a heart attack! I must calm down!" What this did was to add more fear-producing chemicals to those already in your blood and nervous system. What you are doing is "scaring yourself with fear."

So, Marian, I am asking you to submit to your fearful feelings. Let them come. Let them do their worst. They will not injure you. You are not crazy. You will not go crazy. This fear-panic cycle that you have gotten yourself into over time is just a wrong turn that you took in dealing with some of your life problems. We will get to those problems: your relationship to your husband, your dissatisfactions, your feelings of being apart and alienated. But, first, we will get you out of the nightmare of fear control.

With no father and an alcoholic mother who abandoned her at age fourteen, Marian became a self-made woman. She had been working since age eleven to support her mother's drinking and pay the rent. After her mother left, Marian continued to work while attending school. She finished high school and won a four-year college scholarship. She had learned to put impossible demands to succeed on herself.

While in college Marian married and had two children. She and her husband fought and struggled with their attempts to control each other, and over a period of time became so alienated that they divorced.

The habits of self-control and of self-demanding behavior, which Marian had learned over the years, resulted in some struggles with her children. But her intelligence supported her demands. She was able to interact with her children using brilliant feats of reason. They submerged their contrary independent actions so that the family's good interactions were preserved.

Marian learned accounting on her own and became a clerical worker, then an accountant for a manufacturing firm. There she met and married a man with a similar background to her own. He was an extremely conscientious, high-principled man and life was good, but only for a year or so. Marian gave up her job and her husband started his own business. Unfortunately, his business only staggered along while debts mounted.

Marian began to disintegrate. By leaving her job she had become vulnerable. She had no income of her own. She was unable to force her husband into what she felt were necessary decisions through logic though she tried. Such decisions might have helped the company.

Marian's mounting apprehensions led to increased control attempts—demanding, manipulating, driving her husband into guilt trips. She managed only to drive him away. He worked days, evenings and sometimes all night.

Both Marian and her husband became chronically angry, though he seldom complained. She continued to ride him unmercifully, which resulted in her increasing dislike of her own displays of anger. She was well aware of these control attempts and felt bad because of them. She fought off this self-criticism by increased faultfinding with her husband that "justified" her more blatant attempts to attack him. These justifications for her attacks on her husband became a "laundry list" of faults and transgressions on his part. Added to that were the awful consequences which would befall the family as a result of his traits and actions. The worse Marian felt, the more blatant the attacks became. The worse she felt about what she was doing, the more frequently she used the laundry list to justify the attacks. But the laundry list itself was frightening and alienating, which in turn necessitated more attacks which led to the vicious circle.

And then Marian's panic attacks began.

The transition of Marian's anger to fear can be identified in this hypothetical scenario involving her thinking.

From Anger to Fear

Attempts to Control by Attacking	Effects of Attacks
Marian attempts to control husband: "So, you think **you're** suffering? Well, you deserve to suffer! It's you're fault we have no money. You made me give up my job, interfered with the children, made a miserable mess out of the business... and you won't listen to my advice."	These attacks on her husband increase Marian's fears because they are as alarming to her as they are meant to be to her husband.
Marian attempts to control herself: "What am I going to do? The kids need cloths; and I don't have money for the house payment...They're about to repossess the car. I ought to go to work."	This attempt at problem solving is riddled with threats of dire events lurking in her future. These threats raise Marian's fear level and lead her back to attacks on her husband.

"But I shouldn't have to work! He promised to support me! He promised I'd never have to work again! He deserves to be punished! God, how I hate him. I can't stand to have him touch me."

Marian's feeling of alienation is increased by viewing her husband as having broken promises to her; fear increases, leading back to laundry list of tools to control her husband.

"Oh. What's happening to me? I'm so scared. My heart is pounding and my hands are freezing. I feel awful. I can't get sick. Who'll take care of the children? I've got to hang on. But I feel so weak.

"I'd better lie down. Something awful is going to happen! But I can't get sick!"

Marian's alienation is extremely high and with it the sense that she is terribly vulnerable. This results in some physical changes, which naturally accompany feelings of danger. She is in the middle of an exercise in controlling her thoughts and feelings using threatening thoughts. This control struggle gets carried over into an attempt to control the very fear symptoms that were produced by the struggle to begin with.

Both Marian and David, whom we'll discuss next, are subject to the fear-panic cycle. How does this get started?

The fear-panic cycle begins with chronic anger grounded in struggles for control that are producing feelings of alienation. Added to the struggles is the "need" to make oneself feel safe by exerting even more control.

Often, people have a history of seeking out friends and confidants who act as support and reduce the feelings of separation and the attendant fearfulness. These friends, and sometimes counselors, help by assuring troubled persons that they are "normal." Friends can assure these persons that they are attractive people who have many strengths. They may also be assured that their reactions to others with whom they are struggling is justified and that their anger and attacks are quite well founded.

Such reassurances work because they reduce the feelings of alienation and the sense of separation that was intensifying the fear. The reassurance is reinforced by a calm, "in control" conduct of the support person. "I'm acceptable in their eyes, so I must not be some alien misfit," troubled people will think. It is helpful to view this helping person as a kind of "authority on life." That is why older, wiser, more experienced friends are sought out. These people may not in fact be wiser and more experienced than others, but it is helpful to alienated people to view them as such. The more support persons are seen to represent the "real world" of normal people, the more one's fear of not really belonging to that world is reduced.

The "authority on life" role of the confidant that works to reassure the alienated person and validate the anger, operates in reverse if the authoritative counselor, friend, or professional shows signs of pulling away. If support people become impatient or demanding or start avoiding the angry and alienated person, then the very message of belonging and normalcy, which had been useful in countering the person's alienation-related fear, now confirms that fear and increases it.

This "dynamic" can work itself out in many ways, but one common way is for the helping person to "hand off" to someone else. Friends may hand off to ministers. Ministers may hand off to counselors and doctors. Doctors may hand off to mental health units; and often along the line a "hand off" is made to medication. Any of these hand offs can precipitate panic in the alienated person because of its estranging message, which makes reassurance by the next "helper" harder to establish.

Another common sequence arises in a marriage when one person finds a friend of the opposite gender who takes on the role of reducing the fear and alienation associated with a control struggle. This may serve to reduce fear in two ways. First, it reassures angry and alienated persons that they are not unlovable and alien. Second, it often leads to an ending of the marriage, which at least temporarily reduces the control struggle stirring up the fear. This pattern can be easily repeated, and each succeeding relationship is likely to have the weight of the not-entirely-ended previous relationships.

Panic can occur at any of the points at which the control struggle is intensified and alienated persons happen to have (or notice) body sensations that are frightening to them at the same time. This unhappy uniting of alienation, urgency to control, and fear of what is happening to oneself can lead to the transition from interpersonal control struggles to internal control struggles. The resulting increases in fear can then easily form and maintain a vicious circle escalating to panic.

In Marian's case her financial vulnerability was frightening her. Her usual response to fear had been to increase control by making demands on herself or others. In this situation she saw her vulnerability as a result of her husband's getting more outside of her control with every one of her attempts to control him. Unable to control him, she fell back on self-demands. The very attempt to "rely on her self" signaled to her how alone she now felt. This new level of alienation pushed her fear level to new highs, which resulted in noticeable physical sensations. These were frightening but totally uncontrollable, leading to more terrifying forecasts on her part in an attempt to get herself to do something about them. The result was an increase in her symptoms. The vicious circle was formed, which led Marian in only one direction—to panic.

Chapter 10

The "Guilties," Fear, and Remorse

It is important to distinguish between the feeling of guilt and the feeling of remorse. Remorse is a healthy and necessary human reaction to our mistakes. Guilt does not include remorse. In fact, guilt tends to exclude feelings of remorse in favor of escape from ownership of guilty acts.

The feeling of guilt is related to anger and is a kind of fear. David's case in this chapter shows the connection between the anger habit and obsessive guilty feelings and thoughts.

Dear David:

You have come a long way in dealing well with your panic attacks. When you first came to me, you had to have your wife accompany you. You weren't sure you could make it to my office even with her. Now you come here alone.

You hadn't been in a store in ten years. Now, you shop alone. You hadn't been to a movie or a football game in years. Now, you can do both. You were getting more restricted in terms of being confined in a prison of your own making month by month; and now you are getting better.

You have accomplished this turnaround mainly by learning that you need not try to control your fear. You have learned to let your fears come when they occur, and to divert your attention to what is immediately around you instead of to your feelings. By letting your fear be there, instead of trying to control it, you have learned that it recedes over time without your having to "do something" to stop it.

However, David, we still have a lot to accomplish. You have recognized that your biggest problem is in anticipating what is going to happen. When your wife tells you that she is going out of town shopping the next day or the next week, you become frightened and pouty and blame her for "putting you through hell." You want to drive further than you have been doing. But as soon as you think about trying, you become frightened about what may happen, and how you might panic, and what you might do if you did panic.

When you anticipate scary situations, you get right back into your "guilties." You have a whole set of memories about the "bad things" you did as a child and, when you are anticipating your wife being unavailable to you in case you panic, you go through these memories and dwell on them painfully. Many of these memories have to do with things you did as a child while exploring sexual feelings. Others have to do with semi-delinquent stunts, like destroying people's property when you were a teenager. There are times now that you worry about hygiene, like when it bothers you whether you remembered to wash your hands before you sat down to eat dinner or after you handled a lot of money.

*David, these problems are connected to your anger. I know this sounds odd to you. You came to me because you were so frightened. How could anger be a problem? Yet, you **are** aware of your anger at your wife when "she puts you through hell" by letting you know when she will not be available. There is, as they say, much more where that came from.*

It's time to take another step in understanding what you are doing that leads to your guilt feelings and fears. This step consists of recognizing the angry nature of your attempts to control your wife when you anticipate needing her to ward off your fears. You are unaware of most of your anger because it occurs automatically, as a habit. But you recognize your anger at your wife. So, that is what we will examine.

To get there, let's start by going back through some of your history which we have discussed before. David, you grew up in a family that lived and breathed anger. Many times you have told me how critical your grandparents who reared you were of every aspect of life. You grew up working hard, morning, noon, and night. Your grandparents constantly observed how most people are lazy. They instilled in you the idea that if you had time to sit down, then you had time to do something that needed doing. Your grandfather could hardly wait to read the local Saturday newspaper with its list of births, in order to see how many mothers were listed as single parents. Then he would go through his weekly tirade against welfare bums and the immoral state of the world.

Not only did your family find fault with everyone, they were constantly worrying about imminent disasters. If some relative were hospitalized, your grandmother would be on the phone broadcasting the "fact" that he or she was dying of cancer. If you wanted to take the car, you were told that you'd probably wreck it or, at the very least, put irreparable wear and tear on it.

Any business dealings your family had were assumed to be struggles against someone trying to take advantage of them. Anything they bought was declared to be defective. Merchandise was always shoddy. Neighbors had designs on an extra foot of property and had to be watched, so they wouldn't build a fence in the "wrong" place. No man was good enough to marry your sisters. No woman was good enough for you.

In short, David, you grew up in what may be called a "stockade atmosphere." It was your family against the world. You were the good guys and the rest of the world was populated liberally with "the others."

There are three things notable about what it means to grow up in a stockade atmosphere. First, there is always danger "out there." Second, there is always the need to be in an impregnable situation. And third, family control gets exercised by the threat of your being thrown "out there."

The danger out there is something that you have noticed before and that we have discussed. The world becomes a very dangerous place. Every place except home is a region where you may be attacked. We've talked about this before, and it has helped you to see that many of your fear attacks occur when you see yourself as intruding on someone else's domain or property. This happened when you became afraid while cutting a hedge. When we looked at what was happening, it turned out that some of the clippings had dropped on to a neighbor's yard. It helped you to see that your fear could be accounted for by your feeling that you were intruding on the territory of a potential enemy. In fact, there was no danger from this neighbor.

It is this concern over treading on dangerous territory that is the hallmark of your problem. It is called agoraphobia, meaning, literally, fear of Agora. The

Agora in ancient Greek cities was a public open space where people congregated to talk and carry on business. It is the open, public nature of many areas, such as stores and shopping malls that bring about fear reactions in the agoraphobic.

David, given the view that you grew up with, that every place outside of the home stockade was a dangerous one, public places are particularly problematic. It is not clear to you that in a public place you are intruding on someone else's domain or you are not.

Suppose another shopper lays claim to your place in line. Suppose you are seen by this person to be acting inappropriately. You're not sure whether you are going to have to back off from another's claim to these territorial rights or whether you should be prepared to defend your own rights. Because public areas are by nature everybody's and nobody's territory the decision is hard to make. So you rush home to the stockade where you know what your rights are and you know what to do—attack outsiders. The first thing to notice is that the world is made out to be a dangerous place where you must be prepared at all times to attack other people and defend against their attacks.

The second thing to notice about growing up in a stockade environment is that it is very important to have the stockade be impregnable. This means that if you are going to be prepared to attack others, you must be unreachable by others. The situation requires lots of checking to see if you are vulnerable in any way. David, this is what is happening when you get the "guilties." You have a whole checklist of possible chinks in your stockade that would make you vulnerable to attack from others. Naturally, these chinks concern the taboos of the society in which you grew up. These are the faults people attack and make fun of, and over which they reject others. Your concern, when you go back over and over your guilty transgressions of past thoughts and deeds, is whether these guilty deeds make you vulnerable today. Your way of discovering your vulnerability is to think of your deeds and see if they make you feel bad. Each time your review provokes guilt. That is, it scares you. You "prove" each time that, yes, you are vulnerable. Your memories of what you did as a child still jolt you with fear. Others could therefore use this whole list of transgressions against you.

*David, what I want you to begin to see is that your guilty thoughts are pro-
duced by you; and they are in preparation for an attack on others. You do not
need to be guiltless if you are not expecting to battle others. The biblical quote,
"He that is without sin among you, let him first cast a stone…" has a reverse
side—"If you don't intend to cast stones, past sins are your own business." You
may wish to make amends or in other ways repent past behaviors, but you need
not be frightened by your past. And most important, you need not keep
rehearsing the past in order to see if you still feel frightened by it.*

*David, the stockade mentality with which you grew up was a natural out-
come of your family's struggle to control everything and everyone around them.
They made the whole world their business. They took personally every story in
the paper and on the evening news. Their habitual anger in the form of criticism and attacks represented their attempts to change things by demanding
that they change. They were prone to temper tantrums, which were aimed at
anything they saw as needing change. These demands were in the form of ver-
bal attacks and judgments, which then required a "stockade" of their guiltless-
ness to be maintained.*

*So, the first thing to remember is that the world is not all that dangerous if
you are not in the attacking business. And the second thing is that, if you
intend to attack (or control) others, you must be invulnerable. By reviewing
our past sins, we find that we're vulnerable and, in the process, we frighten
ourselves. But, if we don't intend to attack, we don't need to review our sins for
that purpose. This, by the way, leaves us free to review our behavior as a preparation for change in order to live a more satisfying life. The past can never be
changed. But our futures can be different from our past if we are free to learn
from our past misdeeds instead of having to hide them.*

*The third thing I want you to notice about the stockade atmosphere in
which you grew up is the way in which family members controlled each other.
Consider what is the worst thing that can happen to someone who lives in a
stockade where everyone outside is considered a potential enemy. The worst
thing is to be thrown out, to be considered one of "them," the outsiders. The*

threat that was held over your head as a child was to be considered one of "the outsiders," one of "those lazy, immoral good-for-nothings."

*If you earned two dollars, you were expected to save two dollars—and you did. If you had ten minutes, you were expected to find something that needed doing—and you did. You learned to work hard and long and pretend you liked it. But you didn't like it and that is the key. You never liked it because you never felt any part of your life was your own. It would be easy to say that it wasn't. It would be easy to say that your behavior was under your family's control. That their ability to threaten you with a demotion to outsider status in order to make you do what they wanted is what constituted their control over you and made your behavior belong to them, not to you. But do you think they felt **their** behavior was under their control? Don't you suppose they felt the need to protect themselves and anticipate the counter moves of others? Weren't their lives as involuntary as yours?*

Yet you maintained a part of you that was yours. It was secret and sneaky, but it felt like you. It was also the basis of your guilt, your laundry list of badness, which constantly needed laundering but never got clean.

Now, David, you have something entirely new to learn. You are not that secret, guilty person that has felt like "you" all these years. In order for you to learn this and see and feel yourself for who you are, you must discover a painful fact. That is the fact of your attempts to control others through threats and anger and judgments, just as your grandparents attempted to extend control. You see, David, you live in a control struggle with your wife. The emotionality you feel as fear, when she gives some indication that she might not be where you can depend on her, begins with anger, an impulse to attack her in order to control her. In order to change the way you feel I'm asking you to look for that anger.

When you are able to identify that anger day in and day out, with every frustration, with every irritation, you will see that you, yes you, bought into your family's stockade mentality. You will be able to see that you have adopted a goal of which you have not even been aware. You are trying to control others by attacking them. And you adopted that goal as a child by identifying safety as a position from which you could always attack others.

Safety, David, is extremely important to people, whether they are children or adults. But it is nearly impossible to obtain safety if we add to the ordinary problems of remaining safe the problems arising from attacking others. If we are always prepared to poke a hornet's nest, we must always wear protective clothing and constantly check it for gaps.

*When you become aware that this is what you are doing, you can change this long-standing goal. If you don't feel you have to control everything around you, you will not have to take a fight stance. You will not have to worry about vulnerability. This means your guilt will change form from fear to remorse, which you can look at and respond to appropriately. Your fear, in turn, will change form from a nameless dread to an alert to what is "out there." Now you can actually seek and find the danger, which is producing your fear. We need our sensibilities in order to feel remorse and fear. Sensibilities are more important than our senses, our eyes and ears, in living our lives with an awareness of what we do and the consequences we bring about. We do not need, in fact we are harmed, by the form of remorse we call guilt that is a frightening sign of vulnerability to attack. We also do not need, and are harmed by, fear which is, itself, frightening because it signals vulnerability **inside** ourselves rather than danger **outside**.*

David, you have felt it the wrong way around all these years. You've known that you wanted to control your wife, but you thought that control was all you could depend on to get her to help you deal with your fears. It's the other way around, David. You have fears and guilt because you try to control others. The missing link that has fooled you is that you missed seeing your own anger in the form of your preparations to avoid attacks. Our goal now is for you to become aware of that anger and to see that you need not be a pawn, driven by it. It is not a force that is driving you. We are trying to find a set of behaviors and thoughts that are merely habits. Together we may refer to them as the anger habit.

You can find these behaviors, look at them, and unlearn them if you decide they are "bad habits." I think you will see as an attractive bargain the exchange of panic for an awareness of danger, which you can do something about. You can also find the exchange of fearful guilt for remorse from which you can learn.

An Example of What David Has to Learn

Earlier, David was driving to the Mall to pick up some groceries at the supermarket. As he pulled into the parking area, he noticed that it seemed to be full. He began to feel frightened and slowed down. Then three events occurred in rapid succession: a car was backing out of a slot; another car was approaching him from his left, and he thought the driver might have noticed the opening; and a police car was cruising slowly toward him down the aisle.

David's Response Choices

David's Response

"There's a place! Oh, no, maybe that fellow has seen the spot too."
Fear mounts. Memories of arguments he has had flooded over David, increasing his fear. He breaks out in a cold sweat. Images of adolescent lawbreaking rear up as memories.
"Oh! There's a cop! He's looking at me! I've got to get out of here!"
David slams on his brakes, backs up, turns the car, and races out of the lot toward home. The police car begins to follow him and his panic grows.

Alternative Response

"There's a place! And here's another car! Remember, I'm trying to park the car so I can shop, not control anybody or prove anything. I'll pull into the spot if it's still there, otherwise find another.
"There's a cop. Good! This place is safe. Or is it? Maybe they've had cars stolen. Remember to lock up.
"Ah-h. The spot is still there. Now to park and find what I want."

Obsessive thoughts concerning past misdeeds are part of the repair work we do to our stockades, the invulnerable places from which we can launch attacks. When a family shares a stockade, as we've seen, they tend to use threats of ouster from the stockade in order to control each other. This can result in panicky concern accompanied by guilty thoughts and worry about past deeds, as we saw with David.

Leaving the stockade was a difficult task for David. It meant recognizing and unlearning his anger habit. It also entailed learning to feel safe while having fun, or while taking breaks from work. Fun and rest were "dangerous" activities in his family's stockade because they were easily attacked as "worthless," participated in by the "bums" outside. As David's agoraphobia faded, he was able to enter the "Agora" again, a place not only for doing necessary life tasks, such as shopping, but also a place for fun and social exchange.

Chapter 11

Voluntary Living

We got to know Rick in Chapter 3, noting that the struggle for control can contribute to a sense of self-importance which is distinct from, and harmful to, self-esteem.

Now we return to Rick, who was angry but didn't know it, and who represents a model of obligatory living. Resolution of Rick's problem will lead toward the state we all desire; namely doing more of what we do because we want to do it. That is voluntary living.

Dear Rick:

You have become more aware of what others do that triggers anger in you. The casual remark, which you see as a put-down, by your boss or your girl friend, makes you angry. And when you ask yourself, "What did I want from them?" you see that you wanted them to give you more respect.

What these others are doing, Rick, is disturbing your sense of self-importance. Self-importance is very delicate; and we are very sensitive to disturbance of it. Our reactions can go from a simple uncomfortable sense of offense and anger, when someone pushes his or her way in front of us in line, to an extreme and lifelong sense of humiliation because a classmate in third grade, who we thought was friendly, made fun of us on the playground for not being completely toilet trained.

I've told you that self-importance is a proclamation of value not provided by our special individuality but, instead, by our identification with a special group. If I'm not too sure of my value to my clients as a provider of help in exchange for the fee they pay me, I can rely on my professional degree by insisting that I be known as "Doctor." This implies that I am an expert who has special knowledge, which flows from my profession and is beyond the grasp of untrained people. I can outfit my office in walnut paneling and lead my clients in all sorts of ways to believe that I am a prestigious member of an elite and highly valued fraternity of exclusive practitioners.

*But using my membership in the community of professionals **in this way** represents a misunderstanding of my membership. Being a professional implies that others can expect me to be competent. I have a responsibility to **be** competent as a result of membership. My membership entails responsibility, not entitlement.*

*An alternative to this "front" of importance is to rely on being a trader. In this case we do not attempt to possess anything from others without payment to them of some kind, and at the same time, which they are unwilling to voluntarily trade to us. It is my self-importance that **demands** that you seek me out as your counselor. You **must** do so because I'm so wonderful that you just have to come to me. My self-esteem resides in the possibility of helping you, which results in my willingness to talk with you if you are willing to pay me to do so. Self-importance demands; self-esteem trades.*

The demands that self-importance makes on others feed the anger habit. We can go a long way toward awareness of angry demands on others and, to some extent, give up the anger habit. But our self-importance will rekindle the anger habit when we least expect it. The casual remark which punctures a pretense or the intentional taunt of a child that says, "you're not such hot stuff" begs us to attack and reclaim what is owed to us by right of self-importance.

But you rightly point out that there must be more to life than just trading. You're right. We have all received more from each other and from the world by far than we have earned. Recognizing this fact as a profound truth is the lock that must be opened to allow us to give up our self-importance, the lock on the door to living a voluntary life.

The key is the realization that no one owes us anything just because of who we are. Neither do we owe anyone anything—not our parents, not our spouses, not even our children—just because of who they are. What we give others, outside of contractual obligation, we give voluntarily, because we want to, because it gives us satisfaction. They owe us nothing in return. After all, if we give to the people in our lives because their importance commands it or decide they owe us in return, how could it have been a gift? It would be a transaction. That idea is contrary to everything you believe.

I know you aren't really convinced that you feel "self-important." That phrase sounds to you like someone such as the First Lady or someone who lives in a big house in Beverly Hills. You don't see yourself like that, Rick, and in fact you aren't like that. The last thing you would do is try to display wealth or power or make a spectacle of yourself, although there are many people whose self-importance takes them in that direction. Your instinct is to do just the opposite. You would much rather be unnoticed, or, as we have talked about several times, aloof. But I think I can reveal your self-importance, now that you recognize your anger when others slight or make fun of you.

If self-importance is not simply self-aggrandizement and delusions of power, what is it? Rick, it consists of a mistake we make about what is given to us. From the time we are born others give us care, concern, and love. Our world consists of, for the most part, people responsive to our needs. Our parents and other family members, as well as our teachers and our community, are not only responsive to us but take an active interest in our welfare without our having to pay for their interest in any way. The psychoanalyst Erich Fromm labeled this caring by others, particularly our mothers, as "unconditional love." That's a good name for it. It is unconditional in that we did not arrange for it and do not need to pay for it. In fact, Rick, we cannot arrange to pay for it because it's a gift.

*As soon as we think of it as paid for, the gift disappears; and that is the mistake we make. We think that what others have freely given us **was** paid for by us. It is this belief —that others are paid by us for their caring and concern— that constitutes our self-importance. If people don't give us concern and deference, we feel cheated and deprived of the payment our self-importance should have required of them.*

You can see now why I refer to it as self-importance. Who is an important person? Important persons are those to whom we need to yield because they have the power either to hand out favors or to make our lives miserable. Well, self-importance is the belief that others love us or defer to us or show caring for us because of our importance. What we have done is to mistakenly assume that what was given to us was instead earned by something about us that pays for their caring. This is our power to make them happy or unhappy.

The claim we make to control others through our importance is often made in a very subtle way. It is made through our relationship identities. By this I mean any name we may call ourselves, which relates us to one person in the world or to a restricted group of people in a special way. Rick, you are a "son," which means there are two people in the world, your parents, with whom you have a special relationship. You are also a "lover," "brother," "friend," "supervisor," "employee," and "patient." All of these "names" indicate some special set of "importances" to you, some set of entitlements to which you have access.

*Now, here is the mistake you make, Rick. You assume, and have assumed all these years, that these relationships must be bought and paid for by you. Your parents have given you a lot, but you have given back to them as a son. You think you have given to them as a trade, not just by what you have done for them but also by **being** their son. Jill, your lover, gives you a lot, but you give her at least as much, and most of the time more, because after all you are her lover and **she earns** by giving to you. Your friendships, past and present, produce the same rewards.*

*Giving in order to receive is an important function. **But that doesn't mean others get something in exchange for everything they do for us.** This view of our relationships makes gifts impossible. It turns all our interactions into transactions, into "let's make a deal." Yes, we make deals with others. We must have agreements and the corresponding obligations they entail. You and Jill must have arrangements concerning the bills and appointments you keep with each other and that influence the important issues like sexual fidelity. But that doesn't mean **all** of your interactions are deal related. When such interactions are* *seen by you in that light, they naturally feel like obligations to you; and when you don't get what you expect from them, you feel they aren't giving what they owe to you and that feeling triggers and "justifies" your anger.*

Rick you connect a lot of your unhappiness to the fact that your life seems to be made up of obligations contained in your relationships. You feel that you must fulfill these obligations whether you want to or not. If you don't fulfill them, you feel guilty. This perceived set of arrangements makes your life a drag. You feel as if everything you do is involuntary, and most of what you would **like** *to do is bad and makes you feel guilty.*

What I want you to do, Rick, is to re-examine these self-important names you have. "Son" is the most important one because it was the first, but "patient" is a more recent one, which involves me, so I'd like you to start there. I'd like you to consider what you have given to me **in exchange** *for what I have given you. Don't consider everything we have given each other, but what have we* **traded** *for. What is our* **arrangement***?*

When you first started with me I said that I would make this hour available to you every week. I would be here, and I would not harm you, and when I felt I could say something that would help you, I would do so. In exchange, I expected you to pay me for these hours unless you canceled or changed your appointment more than twenty-four hours ahead of time. We agreed on this arrangement.

I have kept my part of the arrangement; and you have kept yours. But you have challenged it several times. Remember the time you called a half-hour before your session to change the appointment? You said you had gotten a late start and the hour drive would put you here way late. I said "no," I would not reschedule. You could come for however much time you would have or not come at all. You were angry, but you paid me for the full hour. You kept your part of our arrangement and I kept mine.

Many other times you stopped talking during the hour, or questioned me, and I might or might not say anything. In the beginning you would attack yourself if I didn't say anything or didn't answer you. You would feel confused and dumb and "like a child." But when you started discovering your anger, you would direct your anger at me and pout. Then, a few times, you attacked me verbally and tried to get me to argue with you about my responsibilities as a therapist when I would answer, "I have nothing to say" or was just silent.

Clearly Rick, you expect a lot more from me than my presence and my comments, and you get angry when you don't get it. You do get a lot more from me than my presence. But you don't arrange it. I speak when I have something I want to say. What I say and when I say it is not part of our arrangement. I have not allowed you to control that. It is part of what I do as your therapist. I say to you those things that I want to say. I'm at our hour each week because you paid for the time, but I speak because I want to.

*What I want you to see, Rick, is that what we have arranged to receive from each other is really quite simple. What we have received from each other that we did not arrange is a whole lot more and is free to both of us. As a "therapist" I do my thing because I like it. I've received a lot from you because you give me the opportunity to do what I do as a therapist. You present an ongoing array of problems, which I have to think about, and I like to think about them. They challenge me. I enjoy our exchanges. Along the way, while listening to you, I've learned lots about banking, which you know a lot about, and also about some of your hobbies. I haven't paid for any of this. All I have to do is to be here, for which you pay me, and do my job, which I like to do. I thank you for what you have **given** me.*

What you have received from me has been helpful to you in many ways. Your life is freer as a result. You are less angry. You are a great deal less depressed. But my part in helping you was not arranged by you. You merely paid me for my time, which I delivered; and you received the benefit of what I enjoy doing. We both, in a very profound sense, have received a "free lunch."

Now, let's go back and look at your guilt reactions when I "wouldn't" talk to you, and your anger reactions that came later. Both of these resulted from judgments of yours about our relationship. The guilt reaction—"I'm dumb," "I'm confused," "I don't know what I'm doing"—resulted from a judgment you made which said, "My therapist isn't giving me what I want because I'm a bad patient." Later your anger when I refused to reschedule you was, "My therapist isn't giving me what I deserve as a good patient."

That is the connection, Rick, between self-importance and anger. Your sense of being "a good patient" is equivalent to believing that you arrange what you receive from me. This means that being a good patient makes my behavior, as your therapist, your business. You then demonstrate that my behavior is your business by attempting to control it by attacking me (your anger) when I don't fulfill your expectations.

When you judge yourself to be a "bad patient," you attempt to remedy this by attacking yourself. So, your anger habit comes into play whenever your self-important role as "patient" doesn't get what you expect. You either attack yourself for not being a "good patient" or you attack me for not being a good therapist. We will talk more about this pattern in your other self-important roles, especially "son" and "lover." But for now, let's stick with our relationship.

What I do as a therapist, other than keep my agreements with you, must be done freely by me. Rick, your importance to me is my business. You cannot control that. You cannot control another person's free action by attacking the person. Also, you cannot control your own free action by attacking yourself. You cannot force voluntary behavior. That is why you cannot arrange what you freely get from me. It is also why you cannot get free spontaneous behavior from yourself by self-judgment and self-attack. You get compliance if you are successful; defiance if you're not. But you never get what you want—control over what, by its nature, must be voluntary.

The lesson here, Rick, is not "Don't ever get upset with me or yourself." Distress is a natural product of living. The lesson is not "Don't ever judge me or yourself negatively when a promise is made and not kept." Judgment is the natural product of an unfulfilled obligation.

The lesson is "Don't assume that all your interactions with people who are important in your life consist of a deal which implies an obligation." Interactions need not be transactions. The place I'm asking you to begin seeing this is right here in our sessions. We have a very simple "deal." Our transactions consist of my time and promise not to injure you, that is, to provide a safe place for you to interact with someone openly for your payment. This means that I'm obligated to be here and not to attack you or use you. Beyond that, whatever I say and do is "interactional"; that is, voluntary, and is done for my own reasons. I will not submit to your demands, as you have seen. Whatever help I can give results from what I do for my own reasons and what you do for yours. One of my reasons is that I like you and enjoy seeing you happy rather than miserable. Another is that I like doing what I do. In either case the reasons are mine and my business. What you receive from this is free. It is yours without conditions. It is unconditional.

*I'm happy minding my own business because it allows me to act voluntarily most of the time. Not **all** the time. I must make some agreements with others and then keep them whether I want to at the time or not. But those agreements, although very important, are not my whole life or even a large part of it. When others do not live up to their agreements with me, I have occasion to demand that they do so. But these occasions are rare.*

I think when you sort out the agreements you need to make with others from what you and others do voluntarily and understand these fully, you will find it easier to give up the anger habit. You will feel the need for angry demands much less often; and your most important reward will be to feel a sense of voluntary living returning to your life.

Rick lived a "well-ordered" life: Up at 7:00, to the bank where he worked by 8:30, leaving at 5:00 to stop off for one beer at the tavern

[***Therapist***: "Why?"

Rick: "I dunno. I just always do."]

Watch TV with Jill until 11:00 except Friday.

[***Therapist***: "What about Friday?"

Rick: "That's movie night."]

Make love to Jill Tuesday, Friday and Sunday morning.

[*Therapist*: "Why those times?"
Rick: "Well, she expects me to."]
Call his mom on Sunday.
[*Therapist*: "Why on Sunday?"
Rick: "She expects it.]
Roses on Jill's birthday; a plant at Easter.
[*Therapist*: "Why?"
Rick: "That's what people do! Besides, she expects it."]
Therapist: "Any change in your depression?"
Rick: "No. Same as always. Life is such a goddamn drag."
Therapist: "What would happen if you broke the pattern?"
Rick: "What do you mean?"
Therapist: "What if you were feeling warmly toward Jill and made a sexual advance on, say, Saturday morning or Sunday night or the middle of Saturday afternoon? Or, what if you took her to a jazz club on Wednesday evening or went out for breakfast on Sunday morning?"
Rick: "She'd blow her top! I tried it once when we woke up on a workday. She called me a goddamn lech! Made me mad all day!

"Then we had a big argument that night. She punished me all week long. Every time, she had a headache. And she kept saying, 'You don't love me,' and 'All you want is my body!' No thanks. I'll keep to what she expects."
Therapist: "Does her expectation result from an agreement you two have made about when to have sex or is it merely based on what has happened in the past?"
Rick: (pause) "Okay. So you're getting at whether our sex life is a transaction or an interaction."
Therapist: "What would the difference imply?"
Rick: "Well let's see. (Laughing) I guess we both know what it would imply if it were a transaction. But seriously, if it is a transaction, then we are both obligated to have sex at certain times. If it is an interaction, then

it is voluntary. I know neither she nor I want to make love if it feels like a duty to either of us."

Therapist: "But, you feel 'compelled' *not* to approach her?"

Rick: "That's true. That doesn't feel voluntary at all. You're telling me that I act out of obligation, that I do everything to avoid guilt or that I avoid being attacked by acting predictably.

"And you're telling me that when I act unpredictably with Jill, I shouldn't take her anger personally. I'm just trying to protect my feeling that how she views me is the only thing I have going for me. So if she calls me a 'lech,' I've got nothing.

"But you're also implying that the feeling of obligation is causing my depression, making me feel angry all the time. So I have to let down my guard. I have to break away from the goal of protecting my 'reputation' with others and especially with Jill. What you call my self-importance. I'm not trying to hurt anyone. I'm not even demanding anything from her.

"All of a sudden I feel so goddamn free. Where did all that come from?"

Therapist: "You."

The last exchange with Rick illustrates a central benefit of recognizing the habit of anger, an increase in the sense of living life voluntarily.

Transactions occur between independent individuals or groups when both sides have something of value to trade. One buys and the other sells when money is involved or an exchange of items of value is consummated. In either case the relationship between the parties consists of and is defined by the exchange. The proper remedy for a "breach of contract" may very well include some form of demand or attack. All stable relationships have some transactional element. The marriage "contract," the employment agreement, your mortgage with the bank, all make certain behaviors obligatory and therefore involuntary once they are entered into. Difficulties arise when those few obligations, which are a part of a relationship in the beginning, start to multiply and become a major share of the relationship and of the lives of those concerned. How does this happen?

Interactions occur when two or more parties give and take voluntarily as independent units within a system over time. Each is empowered to give freely of himself or herself, and his or her talents, services, or property. Because the system persists over time, each party tends to predict the behaviors of the other. Such predictions tend to distort the voluntary nature of the interaction as each begins to believe that he or she has earned what is received. It is owed. The distortion threatens to reduce the system to a transaction. To maintain a system of independence, each person giving freely, roles must be defined to handle any transactional functions, leaving the interactional functions to operate freely.

What does it mean to live an "involuntary" or "obligatory" life? An Asian student put it this way:

"It seems that my whole life has been involuntary. At home I spent almost all of my time studying. My whole family talks about getting high grades. I must be the best or I will bring dishonor on my family. And I must be the best violist, the most virtuous daughter, the most creative poet… I cannot raise flowers or vegetables for the joy of it. They must take prizes. I am not allowed to fail at anything. Consequently, I have no *joie de vivre*, no joy of living; I live only to avoid pain, guilt and shame. Men? I am twenty-five years old and I have never been with a man. Males exist only to be beaten out for top honors."

And what is voluntary living? It may be anything—and that's the point.

It may mean living dangerously, if you wish, mindful of the consequences and being willing to accept them; or living conservatively, knowing what you're missing and being willing to miss it but deciding for yourself.

It may mean that you work at being invulnerable to petty slights, insults, and jealousies of others; impervious to the power moves of colleagues, politicians, neighbors, petty officialdom. It means that you understand the weakness which drives those behaviors, treating them as the problems of less fortunate others and not needing to take them personally.

It may mean working at owning your values and ideas, trusting your observations rather than accepting authority or adopting "what everybody believes," boldly taking responsibility for your perhaps unpopular beliefs, and being willing to "suffer the slings and arrows of outrageous fortune" because they are part of the price of living the voluntary life.

It may mean not expecting or demanding thanks from others, nor appreciation, nor gratitude from those who benefit from your good works, and then fully experiencing **their** gifts of thanks and gratitude when and if they are freely given. Those behaviors are their business; and your good works were given freely. It may mean acting constructively, solely for the satisfaction of knowing that you are being constructive.

It may mean "taking time to smell the roses" because they are there; and opening your senses to both the joys and the pain of others, doing what you can to increase the joys and to reduce suffering without being dismayed that you can't eliminate it completely or forever.

It may mean feeling free to share your beliefs, ideas, talents, skills, and physical favors with whoever is receptive, mindful of both the short-term pleasure and the long-term pain that may result, but to share without fear while mindful of the past with both its joy and its remorse.

It may mean being guided by rational thought when embroiled in others' emotionality, but also being guided by emotions when there is no basis for rational thinking and accepting the outcome, no matter how devastating, since it was the best that could be done.

Voluntary living may mean working on recognizing criticism ("constructive" or not) as an attack and examining it for whatever information it may contain, then dismissing it.

Whatever voluntary living may mean for you, it cannot be yours if you remain in the grip of the anger habit. The automatic response to your unmet expectations with angry demands will blind you to the possibilities of giving freely to others and receiving gratefully from them.

A voluntary life is a balance between obligation and freedom of your own creation. Choosing your arrangements with others, which result in obligations, is up to you. The rest of your life remains free.

Chapter 12

Choices Beyond the Anger Habit

Extreme anger and aggressive behavior are so difficult to treat clinically that, given our human capacity to feel these emotions, our negative reactions often seem unavoidable. We do not view interpersonal and internal conflict as an inevitable part of living. Instead, we view emotionality (distress) as merely a signal that our predictions (expectations) are not correct. We view angry feelings as information and we prepare attacks as our method of enforcing these predictions.

It is the very presence of our angry feelings, if we recognize them that gives us a chance to reconsider the path we are on and to choose another course of action. The authors view most of what is seen and experienced as anger as being a bad habit. That habit takes us automatically and unthinkingly to an attempt to rule our world and ourselves by making demands, backed by angry displays.

Most of what is commonly seen and labeled as anger (aggressive language and overt attacks), as well as most of what is experienced as anger (angry thoughts), are really habitual behaviors. These began before we were old enough to know any better way to reduce distress. They were reinforced in later struggles with others. The behaviors and feelings we are aware of as anger are only the tip of the iceberg. Most of our attempts to control others, that is, most of our anger habit, are below our awareness. We are unaware, not because the anger habit is an instinct in our unconscious but because its occurrence is so over learned that it operates automatically. This vast collection of habitually angry actions in response to unmet expectations is the core of our irrational demands on ourselves and others.

Our lack of awareness of anger, its unconscious existence, makes us emotionally blind to our judgments, criticisms, aloofness, self-importance, and ideas of control. These are all forms of attack or preparation for attacks on others or ourselves.

The primary way to overcome the human problems described in the cases in this book is to help individuals become aware of their criticisms, judgments, self-importance, and aloofness as attacks and preparation for control. Then they must become aware that their unhappiness is at once an outcome of their angry and controlling approach to themselves and others, and also an essential part of that effort.

The unhappiness, which brings many clients to seek help from a counselor, consists of some combination of anxiety, inability to experience pleasure, and guilt. Clients bring both their unhappiness and the "solutions." These are aloofness, efforts to control themselves and others, and attempts at self-importance, which are blotting out self-esteem.

Clients want to give up their unhappiness by enlisting the therapist's help in making these "solutions" work. Clients want to rid themselves of anxiety by increasing control and ask for the therapist's aid in doing so. Clients wish to increase pleasure by becoming more detached from those they cannot control, and seek the therapist's help in order to live more happily by getting the therapist to agree that others have made them miserable.

But the answer to the clients' unhappiness is altering these "solutions." To reduce anxiety requires that we reduce our preparations for attacking others and ourselves in an attempt to control behavior. It requires that we recognize our preparations to control as preparations to attack. It requires understanding that our preparations to attack are preparations to defend. Our preparations to defend are anticipations of attacks on ourselves; and these anticipations of attack are what we experience as anxiety.

When we prepare for control by seeking a superior (aloof) vantage point, we cut ourselves off from others. The result is that we feel alone and empty. When we prepare for control by judging others negatively, we must prepare to be judged ourselves. Then we feel guilty (fearful of our vulnerability), so we run from our guilt and succeed only in sacrificing our ability to experience remorse. When we succeed in arranging our lives by controlling ourselves through self-attack, we experience the result of control (the loss of our own freedom). That leaves us feeling coerced, lifeless, and depressed.

When we succeed in controlling others by making our interactions into transactions, we lose spontaneous contact with others and feel alone and unloved.

The alternative to using these "solutions" to our unhappiness is to open our eyes to what that unhappiness represents. The capacity to feel is the capacity to sense how and why we act. Anger serves us because it tells us where we are headed. It tells us we are preparing to try controlling others with force.

If you decide to carry on with force, then do it. We may all need to defend ourselves against you if you use force. But consider some alternatives.

An alternative to self-control with self-threats is running amok and "going crazy." But so is self-respect and thoughtful problem solving. An alternative to controlling others is control **by** others. But so is respect for others' rights to self-determination and voluntary interactions with others who are willing to freely share some part of their lives with us. An alternative to attacking others with judgments of their behavior is to surrender our values and to endorse all actions by others. But so is protection of ourselves from the harmful actions of others (by force if necessary), with the understanding that if any meaningful change is to occur in the behavior of these others, it must take place voluntarily.

An alternative to self-importance is to attack ourselves and wallow in low self-esteem. But so is the recognition of what we have to offer that others may wish to share and to enjoy sharing what we have of value with others through either trading or giving.

In summary, the alternative to "The Anger Habit" is not "The Love Habit" or "The Submissive Habit" or any other kind of habit. The alternative to habitual behavior is reasoned behavior. We have no reasonable alternative to our emotionality. It is a necessary part of being a human being. Emotionality, properly understood, enriches our experience of ourselves and our world beyond anything our other senses offer us. To attempt to alter our feelings directly with drugs or indirectly by narrowing our attention to only "good" feelings, degrades that experience.

We do have alternatives for our actions when our feelings tell us we are headed along an undesirable path. To pursue an alternative, reasoned course when our angry feeling tells us we are preparing to attack is not a denial or manipulation of anger. It is a respectful use of the information that anger represents.

A large portion of anger is not emotionality at all. It is a complex set of habitual behaviors stimulated by a misunderstanding of emotionality. The habitual behaviors of judgment, criticism, and strategies for enhancing control through self-importance and aloofness are replaceable once they are recognized for what they are. These replacements—openness to information, self-respect, thoughtful problem-solving, respect for others' lives, voluntary interaction, self-protection, self-esteem, sharing what we have of value—-are behaviors that can result from reasoned consideration of our life circumstances. These replacements need not be made into habits. To do so would be to betray human nature.

To conquer the anger habit leaves open the question of how we live our lives. Choice really does mean choice. It means acting without **automatically** using force or threats of force.

It is a contradiction to force someone to do something and then describe what they did as voluntary. It is a like contradiction to expect that what we do as a result of self-threats will seem voluntary to us. It is the **use of threats**, which can be voluntary and will seem so when it becomes less habitual. The compliant behavior that results from the use of threats, if it occurs, will have been forced and will seem involuntary.

The common complaint that "my whole life is made up of obligations" is a telltale sign that the major part of one's life is made up of transactions, which we feel we must carry out. Individuals fail to see that they are habitually using threats to keep others and themselves in compliance with such obligations. Yet they see all too well that the resulting behaviors seem involuntary. Recognition of the anger habit provides choices in self-management. In some situations one may voluntarily choose to threaten oneself in order to comply with an important value —say, keeping a commitment. The short run consequences of complying are uninviting, but the long-term benefits serve an important result. Even though carrying out the compliant behavior will still seem involuntary, the act of choosing self-threats **is** and will seem voluntary.

Self-management without **automatic** threats may very well result in a re-thinking of the number and value of our commitments so as to live a more satisfying life. But it avoids the wholesale disavowal of all behaviors that seem involuntary. If all commitments are canceled because they can't be kept without "making" oneself keep them, the result is a valueless life in which our behavior is easy prey to loss, depression, and feelings of meaninglessness.

The middle ground —voluntary living—is not a state of living in which force and/or threats are never considered or used. It is a state of living in which the use of force and threats are not **habitually** used. It is the anger **habit**, the habit of attempting to reduce distress by attacks, which is incompatible with voluntary living.

Once we expose our habit of attacking **as** a habit, we have choices to make. After that it's up to each of us.

About the Authors

Carl Semmelroth has maintained a mental health practice for over twenty-five years in Kalamazoo and Coldwater Michigan. He received his Ph.D. in psychology from the University of Michigan.

Donald E. P. Smith, Emeritus Professor of Educational Psychology at the University of Michigan, is the author of six books and numerous journal articles.

0-595-14080-7